Psychiatric Mnemonics
& Cli~i~~~
S~

David J. Robinson, B.A., M.D., F.R.C.P.C.

Diplomate of the American Board of Psychiatry & Neurology

Consultation-Liaison Psychiatrist
St. Joseph's Health Center
London, Ontario, Canada

Rapid Psychler Press

P.O. Box 596305   P.O. Box 8117
Fort Gratiot, Michigan   London, Ontario
USA 48059-6305   **Canada** N6G 2B0

Toll Free Phone 888-PSY-CHLE (888-779-2453)
Toll Free Fax 888-PSY-CHLR (888-779-2457)
Outside U.S. & Canada — Fax 519-657-9753
website: www.psychler.com
email: psychler@psychler.com (editor's email)
          rapid@psychler.com (business manager's email)

ISBN 0-9682094-1-6
Printed in The United States of America
© 1998, Rapid Psychler Press
Second Edition, First Printing

The author assumes no responsibility for the consequences
of diagnoses made, or treatment instituted as a result of the
contents of this book. Such determinations should be made
by qualified mental health professionals. Every effort was
made to ensure the information in this book was accurate at
the time of publication. However, due to the changing nature
of the field of psychiatry, the reader is encouraged to consult
additional sources of information.

Dedication

To my parents, Monty & Lilly, for giving me my first lesson in mnemonics by helping me learn the colors with the use of Smarties.®

Rapid Psychler Press
produces books and presentation media that are:

- *comprehensively researched*
- *well organized*
- *formatted for ease of use*
- *reasonably priced*
- *clinically oriented, and*
- *include humor that enhances education, and that neither demeans patients nor the efforts of those who treat them*

Index

Clinical Assessment Guides & Mnemonics

Mnemonics & Clinical Summaries: Axis I Disorders

Mnemonics & Clinical Summaries: Axis I Disorders

Personality Disorders: Axis II Conditions

Biological Treatments

Biological Treatments

Special Topics

Humor Pages

Other Rapid Psychler Products

Author's Foreword

Psychiatric Mnemonics & Clinical Guides was written to provide a succinct and practical overview of psychiatric conditions. This book was designed to be used by students during clinical rotations and for exam review. The emphasis of the mnemonics is on aiding in the recall of diagnostic criteria from the DSM-IV. The clinical guides include supplemental information in a **bio-psycho-social** format to facilitate this approach to treating psychiatric conditions.

The amount of information required in clinical situations continues to grow exponentially. What has not progressed as far are ways to organize and recall this information. Throughout my studies and teaching, I have found humor and mnemonics to be the two most effective and enjoyable ways of encouraging learning. For this reason, I have used these educational enhancements in this book.

Where possible, I have developed mnemonics that reflect some aspect of the disorder. In the Personality Disorder section, I have included caricatures exaggerating aspects of these conditions. This was not done out of disrespect or disregard for those who suffer from these disorders. Quite the opposite. These conditions are among the most difficult to teach, and I feel the added visual element aids comprehension, retention and recall. Similarly, the extra humor pages at the end of the book were included to add practical examples of how these conditions are manifested. I feel that humor is vital in achieving a sense of balance and perspective that is essential to include in educational material.

It is indeed a privilege to be able to produce a second edition of this book. I am indebted to both new readers and those who purchased copies of the first edition. Thank you for your ongoing support.

This book is intended to complement standard textbooks, not to provide a complete summary of psychiatric conditions.

Dave Robinson

London, Ontario, Canada
November, 1997

Acknowledgments

• **Brian Chapman**, for all your great illustrations, advice, and unfailing enthusiasm in putting my ideas on paper

• **Tom Norry**, B.Sc.N., for your thorough reviews and feedback

• **Monty Robinson**, for your careful review of the text

• **Gabrielle Bauer**, for your excellent, thorough, and timely editing of this book

• **Dr. David Wagner** and **Dr. Bryan Weinstein** for contributing mnemonics

The Rapid Psychlers

• **Nicole & Mark Kennedy**, thanks for the assistance, support and going that one extra step

• **Mary-Ann McLean**, for your love, patience and help

• **Alex McFadden**, for helping with the big jobs, little jobs and being a mean Duke Nukem opponent

• **Monty Robinson**, for your continued assistance and generosity

• **Brad Groshok**, for your outstanding technical support and friendship

• **Brian & Fanny Chapman**, both fine and food artists

• **Dr. Donna Robinson**, promotion, sisterly duties and medical consultant

• **Dean Avola**, marketing advisor

• **Jan Macdonald**, website programmer

References

Diagnostic and Statistical Manual of Mental Disorders, 4th Ed.
American Psychiatric Association; Washington, DC, 1994

Clinical Handbook of Psychotropic Drugs, 7th Ed.
K. Bezchlibnyk-Butler, B.Sc.Phm. & J. Jeffries, M.D.
Hogrefe & Huber; Seattle, 1997

Psychiatric Secrets
J. Jacobson, M.D. & A. Jacobson, M.D., Editors
Hanley & Belfus; Philadelphia, 1996

Synopsis of Psychiatry, 7th Ed.
H. Kaplan, M.D., B. Sadock, M.D. & J. Grebb, M.D., Editors
Williams & Wilkins; Baltimore, 1994

Psychotropic Drugs Fast Facts, 2nd Ed.
J. Maxmen, M.D. & N. Ward, M.D.
W.W. Norton & Company; New York, 1995

Psychiatry for Medical Students, 3rd Ed.
R. Waldinger, M.D.
American Psychiatric Press, Inc.; Washington DC, 1997

Note:
The mnemonics for clinical disorders appearing in this book are based on the DSM-IV. Where possible, the actual wording from the diagnostic criteria was incorporated. Used with permission of the American Psychiatric Association.

Terms appearing in **bold print** can be looked up in standard textbooks for further information.

Psychiatric Mnemonics
& Clinical Guides
Second Edition

Mnemonic comes from the Greek word *mnemon*, meaning "mindful."
Mnemosyne was a Titan, and the goddess of memory in Greek
Mythology. She and Zeus bore nine daughters, called the Muses,
who presided over the arts:

Erato (lyric poetry)	Calliope (epic poetry)	Clio (history)
Euterpe (music)	Melpomene (tragedy)	Urania (astronomy)
Thalia (comedy)	Polyhymnia (religious music)	Terpsichore (dance)

*Every great advance in science has issued from a new audacity of
imagination.*

John Dewey

Psychiatry as a Medical Specialty

Psychiatry is at once a frustrating and fascinating field for both students and practitioners.

It is frustrating in that there are no longer the pathognomonic findings or objective signs found in physical medicine. There is no one single sign or symptom that is unique to a particular psychiatric diagnosis. We cannot rely on a blood test, MRI or laparoscopy to clear up diagnostic uncertainty. Substance use can perfectly mimic any clinical condition so that only time and abstinence will help with the distinction. It is also not possible to isolate the person or other social factors from the illness. A surgical patient, for example, is not likely to be kept in hospital longer because of concomitant depression, but this would be quite likely on a psychiatry service.

Psychiatry is fascinating because it deals with the most basic of human problems — emotion, perception, cognition and behavior. Treating mental illness provides the practitioner with an endless variety because it involves the most complicated entity in the known universe (the human brain that is, not managed care). Whereas most cases of congestive heart failure or glaucoma have set treatment protocols, psychiatric illnesses can and do demand creative and varying interventions.

Psychiatry is an all-encompassing field. Every patient on every service experiences emotional reactions to his or her illness. Convincing a patient to take medications, minimize risk factors and comply with discharge arrangements involves a multi-faceted understanding of human nature.

The exploration of the cause and effect of illness along the "mind-body continuum" is an area still in its infancy. For example, the interplay between emotions and changes in immune and endocrine function is now an established subspecialty in the field.

Psychological factors clearly have an effect on medical conditions, and an understanding of this association helps not only to make us better clinicians (in any field), but better students, teachers, spouses, parents, and indeed, people. Despite its current drawbacks and limitations, psychiatry provides a rich and varied approach to understanding and treating mental illness.

The General Psychiatric Interview

A psychiatric interview elicits information that facilitates a **provisional diagnosis** and **treatment plan**. Investigations, as well as short-term and long-term treatment plans, are developed using a **bio-psycho-social** perspective. An interview outline is as follows:

Identifying Data: age, gender, marital status and living arrangements, race, religion, occupation, means of support, sexual orientation

Presenting Complaint: quote the patient's words where possible

History of Present Illness
• duration and severity of symptoms; course since onset of symptoms
• degree of social and occupational impairment
• precipitating and perpetuating factors for current difficulties
• ask for specific information to get as vivid a picture as possible

Psychiatric History
• previous hospitalizations; duration of stay; involuntary commitment
• types of treatment: medications, ECT, various forms of therapy
• efficacy of past treatments; compliance with treatment; side effects
• prior diagnosis or diagnoses given; history of harm to self or others

Medical History
• presence, course and severity of medical conditions
• use of prescription and non-prescription medication
• alcohol use, recreational drug use, head injuries, pregnancies
• neurologic conditions, environmental exposure, unexplained symptoms

Personal History
• birth complications; developmental milestones; prolonged enuresis
• education: level obtained, special requirements, extracurricular interests
• history of abuse: physical, emotional, sexual, verbal
• legal involvement; military service (type of discharge); institutional care
• occupational and relationship history

Family History
• presence of psychiatric and medical conditions in first-degree relatives
• types of treatment used; effectiveness of treatment
• history of suicides and attempts, neurologic conditions, mental retardation
• substance abuse may have masked symptoms in relatives
• past diagnostic systems were less structured and precise than the DSM-IV

Mental Status Examination
• often considered the "physical exam" or "brain stethoscope" of psychiatry
• inquiries must be made about current suicidal and homicidal intentions

The Emergency Room Interview

A psychiatric interview in the emergency room seeks to answer the question, "*Why is the patient here now?*" The focus is to obtain information that helps determine an appropriate **disposition**. Of particular importance in this decision are the following areas:

• **Presenting Complaint and History of Present Illness**
• **Psychiatric History**
• **Medical History and Substance-Related Disorders**
• **Legal Involvement and History of Dangerousness**
• **Mental Status Examination**

Prior to seeing the patient —
Assess the acuteness of the situation to ensure that this remains the patient's emergency, not yours.

• be aware of the security arrangements available; attend to your safety
• are the police or security guards in attendance or nearby?
• read the emergency chart
• peruse the patient's hospital file for pertinent information
• how was the patient brought to the hospital? (e.g. police, friends, on own)
• is the patient intoxicated, restrained, or being held involuntarily?
• has bloodwork been drawn? (e.g. medication toxicity, ethanol level)
• is an overdose or head trauma suspected?
• is someone available to provide collateral history?
• does someone from the emergency staff have additional information?

When seeing the patient —
The mental status of the patient is of paramount importance. Patients who have perceptual abnormalities, formal thought disorders, or delusions are the most likely to become dangerous. The following suggestions can help minimize the risk of violence:

• don't challenge the patient's beliefs, especially when starting the interview
• give explanations for your actions; demonstrate openness
• respect the patient's autonomy
• maintain your composure
• stress that thoughts and feelings are *verbalized*, not *acted upon*
• allow adequate (even ample) space for patients
• sit close to the exit to facilitate your escape if necessary
• do not block the door should the patient bolt
• seating arrangements may be altered to suit the patient
• introduce others and explain their purpose in the room
• be attuned to your feelings; don't react with anger or sarcasm

The Consultation-Liaison Interview

Consultation psychiatry involves the management of patients in medical or surgical settings. Consultation requests usually involve:

• Problems with cognition — delirium, psychosis, excessive denial
• Problems with affect — anxiety, despondency, apathy, hostility, euphoria
• Problems with behavior — dependency, hostility, non-compliance
• Capacity to consent to treatment and/or manage financial issues
• Acute medical illnesses in patients with chronic psychiatric problems
• Coping strategies/stress management for serious or prolonged illnesses
• Ideas/attempts of self-harm or harm towards someone else

These areas are of special significance in consultation psychiatry:

Hospitalization Particulars
• length of stay prior to consult request
• how did the patient come to medical attention?

Medical/Surgical History
• type, course and severity of the illness
• current treatment and its efficacy
• plans for future investigations and treatment
• what has the patient been told about his or her condition?

History of the Reasons for the Consultation
• precipitating and perpetuating factors
• exacerbations and remissions of behavioral problems
• was anything brought in by visitors? (e.g. ethanol, pills from home, etc.)
• possible association with procedures, interventions, medications, etc.

Medication Review
• psychiatric complications of non-psychiatric medications (e.g. steroids)
• medical problems caused by psychiatric medications (e.g. lithium)
• possible effects of psychiatric medications on pre-existing conditions

Laboratory Investigation Review
• has appropriate testing been carried out and the results reported?
• have serum levels been ordered for applicable medications?
• is there an association between biochemical or hematologic abnormalities and a change in clinical status?

Review of Information
• expand on the admitting history, e.g. substance abuse, family history
• speak to the referring source for information not on the chart
• check the emergency record and all multidisciplinary notes to obtain and corroborate information

The Mental Status Examination (MSE)

The Mental Status Examination (MSE)
is the interview component in which
cognitive functions are tested and
inquiries are made about the symptoms
of psychiatric conditions. It is a set of
standardized observations and
questions designed to evaluate:

• Sensorium
• Perception
• Thinking
• Feeling
• Behavior

The MSE is an integral part of *any* clinical interview, not just one that
takes place in a psychiatric context. An assessment of cognitive
functioning must be made before information from patients can be
considered accurate. *The MSE records only observed behavior,
cognitive abilities and inner experiences expressed during the
interview.* The MSE is conducted to assess as completely as
possible the factors necessary to arrive at a provisional diagnosis,
formulate a treatment plan and follow the clinical course.

The MSE is a portable assessment tool that helps identify
psychiatric symptoms and gauge their severity. With experience, it is
a specific, sensitive, and inexpensive diagnostic instrument. The
MSE takes only a few minutes to administer and yields information
that is crucial to making a diagnostic assessment and starting a
course of treatment.

The MSE can be viewed as the equivalent of a physical exam in
other areas of medicine. A popular approach to a systematic
examination follows the acronym **I.P.P.A.**

• **I**nspection	Further "looking into," "touching on," "sounding out,"
• **P**alpation	and "listening to" is required to fully evaluate
• **P**ercussion	psychiatric symptoms. Both the physical exam and
• **A**uscultation	MSE are recorded separately from the body of the
	history. However, unlike the physical exam, the
	MSE is at least partly integrated with the history.

Components of the MSE

The MSE can be thought of as a psychiatric "review of symptoms." As outlined on the previous page, the assessment of five main areas yields information necessary for a differential diagnosis and treatment plan. Expanding these five areas gives the psychological functions that are assessed and recorded in the MSE.

- **Sensorium & Cognitive Functioning**
Level of consciousness and attentiveness
Orientation to person, place and time
Attention
Concentration
Memory
Knowledge
Intelligence
Capacity for Abstract Thinking

- **Perception**
Disorders of sensory input where there is no stimulus (hallucinations) or where a stimulus is misperceived (illusions), or of disorders of bodily experience

- **Thinking**
Speech
Thought Content (*what* is said)
Thought Form (*how* it is said)
Suicidal or Homicidal Ideation
Insight & Judgment

- **Feeling**
Affect (objective, visible emotional state)
Mood (subjective emotional experience)

- **Behavior**
Appearance
Psychomotor agitation or retardation
Degree of cooperation with the interview

The Mental Status Examination (MSE)

"ABC STAMP LICKER"

Appearance
Behavior
Cooperation

Speech
Thought — **form** and **content**
Affect — visible moment-to-moment variation in emotion
Mood — subjective emotional tone throughout the interview
Perception — in all sensory modalities

Level of consciousness
Insight & Judgment
Cognitive functioning & Sensorium
    Orientation
    Memory
    Attention & Concentration
    Reading & Writing
Knowledge base
Endings — suicidal and/or homicidal ideation
Reliability of the information supplied

 MSE Tidbits

• The MSE can also be considered part of the **objective** portion of the **S.O.A.P.** approach to recording clinical information:

Subjective — Consists of sections from the interview: Chief Complaint; History of Present Illness; Past History (Medical & Psychiatric); Family & Personal History

Objective — Recording of observations: **Mental Status Exam,** Physical Examination, Laboratory Testing

Assessment — Provisional Diagnosis & Differential Diagnoses

Plan — Further Investigations, Short- and Long-Term Treatment

More on the MSE

The MSE is often unpopular for two reasons:
• The questions are difficult to formulate because they are not asked in other types of interviews or in other areas of medicine, psychology, nursing, etc.
• The questions appear to be of dubious relevance.

Once these two difficulties are surmounted, the MSE becomes an enjoyable and interesting aspect of interviewing. To achieve this level of comfort, it helps to realize that almost half of the MSE is obtained "free" through observation and discussion from the initial parts of the interview.

"Free" parameters	Parameters to ask about
Level of consciousness	Orientation
Appearance	Cognitive Functioning
Behavior	Suicidal/Homicidal Thoughts
Cooperation	Knowledge Base
Reliability	Perception
Affect	Mood
Thought Form	Thought Content

Remember, all psychiatric diagnoses are made clinically in interview situations. There is no test or single identifying feature for psychiatric conditions. This emphasizes the necessity for a thorough assessment, of which the MSE is an essential component. A sample MSE report is included on page 149.

MSE Tidbits

• The MSE is also called the Present State Examination (PSE).
• The Mini-Mental State Examination (MMSE) is **NOT** the same as a complete MSE. The MMSE is used to screen for cognitive impairment and does not include several key areas of evaluation
• The MSE consists of a relatively standardized approach and set of inquiries. However, an instructor may have his or her own rationale for doing things a certain way. After getting exposure to as many styles as possible, assimilate this knowledge into an approach that suits you. Different approaches can be used at different times in different ways; there is no one "right" approach.

Integration of the MSE and History

Psychiatric History	MSE Component
• Identifying Data • Chief Complaint	• **Appearance** • **Behavior** • **Orientation** (ask patients for their full name, if they had difficulty finding the room/clinic/hospital) • **Level of Consciousness** (this is usually obvious)
• **History of Present Illness (HPI)** 5 - 10 minutes of relatively unstructured questions using open-ended inquiries and other facilitating techniques	• **Cooperation** • **Speech** • **Thought Form** • **Thought Content** (this open format allows patients to talk about what concerns them, a valuable indicator of thought content)
• **Exploration of Symptoms from the HPI** More focused assessment with elaboration of material from the HPI using closed-ended questions to get more specific information	• **Affect** • **Mood** • **Suicidal/Homicidal Ideation** • **Elements of Cognitive Testing** (it may be convenient to include these components at this point to help gauge the severity of reported symptoms)

Direct Testing of other MSE Components
If certain areas aren't amenable to questions earlier in the interview, specific inquiries must be made at some point to assess these functions
	• **General Knowledge**
	• **Perception**
	• **Insight & Judgment**
	• **Formal Cognitive Testing**
	   Memory
	   Attention & Concentration
	   Reading & Writing
	   Abstract Thinking

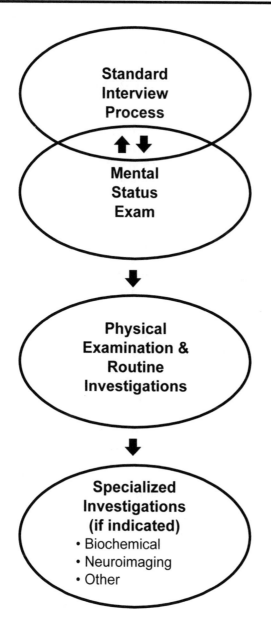

* From the book:
Brain Calipers: A Guide to a Successful Mental Status Exam
David J. Robinson, M.D.
© Rapid Psychler Press, 1997
ISBN 0-9680324-3-5; softcover, 392 pages

The Psychiatric Physical Exam

Feature	Possible Implication*

Head and Neck

• Altered pupil size	Drug intoxication/withdrawal
• Argyll Robertson pupil	Neurosyphilis
• Corneal pigmentation	Wilson's Disease
• Piercing of lips, nose, eyebrows, etc.	Borderline or Antisocial Personality
• Neck mass	Thyroid dysfunction
• Dental caries	Eating disorders (repeated vomiting)
• Nasal septal defect	Cocaine use
• Arcus Senilis	Alcohol use
• Parotid Enlargement	Anorexia/Bulimia Nervosa
• Esophagitis	Eating disorders (from vomiting)

Skin

• Tattoos	Borderline or Antisocial Personality
• Callus/Laceration on knuckles	Eating disorders (due to self-induced vomiting)
• Scars from slashing	Borderline Personality Disorder
• Scars from trauma	Antisocial Personality, Alcohol use
• Needle marks/tracks	IV drug use/dependence
• Piloerection	Opioid withdrawal
• Palmar erythema	Alcohol use
• Bruising	Alcohol use, seizure disorders
• Cigarette burns	Dementia, alcohol use, other neurologic conditions
• Dermatitis or Excoriated skin	OCD — compulsive hand washing, may occur on knees from cleaning in a kneeling position
• Unusual pattern of hair loss	Trichotillomania
• Pretibial Myxedema	Graves' Disease
• Kaposi's Sarcoma	AIDS, HIV encephalopathy
• Lanugo hair	Anorexia Nervosa
• Café au lait macules	Neurofibromatosis
• Red-purple striae	Cushing's Syndrome/Disease
• Edema	MAOI drugs, Anorexia Nervosa
• Spider angiomata	Alcohol abuse/dependence

The Psychiatric Physical Exam

Feature	Possible Implication*
Cardiovascular	
• Mitral Valve Prolapse	Panic Disorder, Anorexia Nervosa
• Hypotension	Anorexia Nervosa
Abdomen and Chest	
• Enlarged liver	Alcohol Use Disorder
• Gynecomastia	Alcohol Use Disorder
• Dilated abdominal veins	Alcohol Use Disorder
• Decreased motility	Pica (with a **bezoar**), Anorexia Nervosa
Genitals	
• Chancre	Syphilis (primary)
• Mutilation	Psychotic Disorder, Paraphilia, Sexual Identity Disorder
• Testicular Atrophy	Alcohol Use Disorder, Anabolic Steroids
Musculoskeletal & Nervous System	
• Gait Abnormalities	Normal Pressure Hydrocephalus Dementia Paralytica (syphilis) High stepping gait (syphilis) Festinating gait (Parkinson's Disease) Alcohol Use (cerebellar degeneration) Wernicke-Korsakoff Syndrome
• Tremor	Parkinson's Disease, lithium use, caffeine intoxication, alcohol withdrawal, anxiety disorders
• Repeated Movements	Tourette's Disorder, Tic Disorders, Autism, Tardive Dyskinesia, OCD, Mental Retardation
• Muscle Wasting	Alcohol Use Disorder

General
• Medic-Alert chain or bracelet

* These implications are speculative. They are not meant to be pejorative or to indicate diagnostic criteria.

Bio-Psycho-Social Management Plan

Assessment in a clinic or outpatient setting	Assessment in an emergency setting
• Admission to hospital? • Outpatient Management?	• Admission to hospital? • Does the patient need to be detained involuntarily?

Investigations

• Biological   Routine physical exam and bloodwork, CXR, EKG
Neuro-imaging (CT and MRI), EEG
Hypothalamic/thyroid/pituitary/adrenal function
Neurologic testing and possible consultation
Special tests: e.g. Dexamethasone Suppression
Test (**DST**), Sleep Studies

• Social   Collateral history from family and other sources
Activities of Daily Living (**ADL**) assessment
Referral to members of multi-disciplinary team

• Psychological   Personality and Intelligence tests
Neuropsychological Test Batteries

Treatment — Short Term

• Biological   Antipsychotics, anxiolytics, mood stabilizers, etc.
Detoxification from medication or substances

• Social   Assistance with housing, finances, etc.

• Psychological   Regular visits, brief therapy (supportive focus),
family meetings, building of therapeutic alliance;
Education and focus/support groups regarding
illness and future treatment

Treatment — Long Term

• Biological   Reduction/optimization of dosage, depot meds
Monitoring of vulnerable organ systems

• Social   Vocational rehabilitation
Community supports and organizations (e.g. **AA**)

• Psychological   Psychotherapy — individual, group, cognitive-
behavioral, psychodynamic, etc.

Treatment Modalities

"ABCDEFGHIJKLM"

Addiction

Behavioral

Cognitive

Drug (medications)

ECT (electroconvulsive therapy)

Family Therapy

Group Therapy

Hospitalization (partial, day or inpatient)

Insight-Oriented (psychoanalysis, psychodynamic psychotherapy)

Job (vocational rehabilitation)

Knowledge (patient and family education)

Leisure (art therapy, music therapy, crafts groups, etc.)

Marital and relationship counseling

Novel treatments (even psychoanalysis was a fad at one point)

 Treatment Tidbits

• Psychotherapy can be defined as the systematic application of a theoretical framework by a trained person in a professional relationship for the purpose of reducing or modifying symptoms, and to promote personal growth and development

• Each form of therapy has its own indications, contraindications, side effects and precautions (even inpatient hospitalization)

• Some treatments work well in combination (such as treating depression with supportive psychotherapy and antidepressants); others do not (such as concurrent individual insight-oriented psychotherapy and group therapy)

• Although there are hundreds of schools of psychotherapy, the broadest subdivision is into those based on psychodynamic principles and those based on behavioral principles

• There are many processes that operate to bring about change in therapy: interpretation, confrontation, clarification, elaboration, etc.

• In order to become a capable therapist, supervision is required

Psychiatric Admission Orders

"A SMART LIST TO RECALL"

Attending Physician/Service

Status (voluntary or involuntary; legal situation regarding admission)
Monitoring (observation level, vital signs, etc.)
Attire (own clothes, hospital pajamas, etc.)
Restraints (chemical, physical, locked room or ward, etc.)
Three Squares (diet — regular, MAOI diet, food allergies, etc.)

Levels (for applicable medications — lithium, carbamazepine, etc.)
Investigations (blood counts, electrolytes, relevant organ testing)
Supplemental information (old chart, signed consents for records)
Tests (if indicated, e.g. EKG, EEG, CXR, CT or MRI scans, etc.)

Therapeutic medications (antipsychotics, antidepressants, etc.)
Other medications (non-psychiatric medications)

Referrals (other medical specialties, psychological testing, etc.)
Evening — hs (bedtime) sedation (commonly requested)
Calming medications (anxiolytics are commonly requested)
Analgesics (commonly requested)
Laxatives (commonly requested)
Letters (to work, school, etc. if needed to account for absence)

Admission Order Tidbits

• Check for medic-alert bracelets and chains
• Ask about food and drug allergies
• Consider leaving an order for anticholinergic medication to treat dystonic reactions when using "traditional" antipsychotics
• Warn patients about expectable side effects if you are starting new medications
• Search patients' clothes and belongings for medications, weapons, electrical appliances, lighters, matches, rope, razor blades, etc.

Dr. Meador's Rules*

7. There is no blood or urine test to measure mental function. There probably never will be.

9. If in doubt about dementia, do a Mental Status Exam.

29. Patients with factitious disease do not remain with the physician who makes the diagnosis.

31. The interview is the beginning of treatment.

60. All patients will lie about something. Some will lie about everything.

133. Let patients ramble for at least 5 minutes when you first see them. You will learn a lot.

135. Listen for what the patient is **not** telling you.

162. Do not talk to an angry patient about any other subject until you understand the source of his or her anger. Take as long as necessary to defuse the anger.

177. Illness behavior attracts attention. All illness has some secondary gain.

215. Factitious skin lesions do not appear between the scapulae.

314. The last statement a patient makes as you leave the room is very important.

333. Think of factitious disorder when there are unusual findings, especially when caring for a physician's spouse or any health care worker.

398. Do not make the error of accepting the first abnormality found as the cause for the patient's symptoms.

421. You cannot diagnose what is not in your differential diagnosis.

* From: **A Little Book of Doctors' Rules**
by Clifton K. Meador, M.D.
Hanley & Belfus Inc.; Philadelphia, PA, 1992
Reprinted with permission.

Assessment of Suicide Risk

"SADDLE SORE WOMAN"

Social isolation
Age
Disturbed interpersonal relationships (**DIRs**)
Drug use/abuse
Lethality of method
Ethanol use

Sex (gender)
Occupation
Repeated attempts
Event — acute precipitant

Will — created or altered
Organic condition — especially serious or chronic medical illnesses
Mental illness — especially schizophrenia and mood disorders
Antidepressants
Note written

 Suicide Risk Tidbits

• The vast majority of suicide victims have a mental illness at their time of death; over half have had an admission to hospital in the 6 months prior to their death
• AIDS, temporal lobe (partial-complex) epilepsy, neurological injuries (head and spinal cord), and progressive neurologic conditions (Multiple Sclerosis, Huntington's Chorea, Parkinson's Disease, etc.) are medical illnesses highly correlated with completed suicide
• A decreased amount of serotonin has been found in the brains of suicide victims; other biochemical abnormalities have been reported
• There may be a genetic component to suicide; hopelessness is the best emotional predictor of future suicide
• Patients do not become suicidal because of interview questions — **ALWAYS ASK**

Assessment of Violence Risk

"ARM PAIN"

Altered state of consciousness (e.g. delirium, intoxication)
Repeated attacks — history of violence
Male gender

Paranoia (in schizophrenia, mania, or delusional disorders)
Age — more likely to be violent if younger and impulsive
Incompetence — due to brain injury, mental retardation or psychosis
Neurologic diseases — e.g. Huntington's Chorea, Dementia

Diagnoses Most Commonly Associated with Violence

"MADS & BADS"

Mania — due to impulsivity, grandiosity and psychotic symptoms
Alcohol — intoxication and withdrawal states
Dementia — diminished judgment and behavioral disinhibition
Schizophrenia — due to command hallucinations or delusions

Borderline Personality Disorder — intense anger, unstable emotions
Antisocial Personality Disorder — disregard for the safety of others
Delirium — hallucinations or delusions can cause violent reactions
Substance Abuse — intoxication, particularly with hallucinogens

Violence Potential Tidbits

• Always be concerned with the potential for violence; most mental health care professionals are assaulted at least once
• Interview rooms should never be locked when in use; rooms can be customized for safety — desks bolted down, emergency alarms, unbreakable glass, heavy objects removed, etc.
• Crisis intervention strategies should be practiced regularly

Medical Differential Diagnosis

"MASTER THIS SCID"

Metabolic
Autoimmune
Septic/Infectious
Traumatic
Endocrine
Renal

Toxic
Hematologic/Circulatory
Idiopathic
Structural

Somatoform (Psychiatric)
Congenital
Iatrogenic
Degenerative

> The SCID stands for the
> *Structured Clinical
> Interview for the DSM-IV*

"VITAMIN CDE"

Vascular
Infectious
Traumatic
Autoimmune
Metabolic
Idiopathic
Neoplasm

Congenital
Drug Induced (Iatrogenic)
Endocrine

Psychiatric Differential Diagnosis
"OF SIG'S SPACED CAMPS"

Other Conditions that may be a focus of clinical attention
Factitious Disorders

Sleep Disorders
Impulse-Control Disorders
Gender Identity Disorders
Sexual Disorders

Somatoform Disorders
Personality Disorders
Anxiety Disorders
Cognitive Disorders
Eating Disorders
Dissociative Disorders

Conversion Disorders
Adjustment Disorders
Mood Disorders
Psychotic Disorders
Substance-Related Disorders

 DSM Tidbits

• The DSM uses five axes to make a complete diagnostic summary:
  • **Axis I**: Major Psychiatric Syndromes or Clinical Disorders
  • **Axis II**: Personality Disorders and Mental Retardation
  • **Axis III**: General Medical Conditions
  • **Axis IV**: Psychosocial and Environmental Problems
  • **Axis V**: Global Assessment of Functioning (GAF Score from 0-100)
• The DSM also uses Axis II to record prominent personality traits and defense mechanisms
• If a General Medical Condition causes a mental disorder, it is coded on Axis I as "(psychiatric disorder) due to (causative medical condition)"; the medical condition is coded on Axis III

Important Organic Considerations

"TIME WON'T PASS"

Trauma — particularly head injuries and intracranial bleeding
Infections — especially of the CNS
Multiple sclerosis
Epilepsy

Wilson's Disease — an inherited defect in copper metabolism
Obstruction of CSF — Normal Pressure Hydrocephalus (NPH)
Nutritional — e.g. vitamin deficiencies, protein-deficient diets
Toxic — ingestion of medication, heavy metals, chemicals

Porphyria, **P**heochromocytoma
Axis of hypothalamus-pituitary-thyroid-adrenals
Space-Occupying Lesions
Substances — abuse, tolerance, intoxication and withdrawal states

 Organic Tidbits

• A correlation between the time course of psychiatric and medical signs and symptoms is especially important to investigate
• First-episode psychosis warrants a complete investigation
• New-onset psychiatric illness late in life often has an organic basis
• There is no single pathognomonic sign or symptom for psychiatric conditions; any of the criteria used in diagnosing psychiatric illnesses can be caused by medical conditions
• Auditory hallucinations, and to a lesser extent visual hallucinations, are symptoms of psychiatric illnesses; hallucinations in other senses warrant an investigation for organic causes
• CT scans are indicated for imaging intracranial calcification, cerebral hemorrhages and tumor margins
• MRI scans provide superior resolution over CT scans; they are particularly useful for MS and other demyelinating diseases and for imaging the posterior fossa and brain stem
• *The body can have as many diseases as it pleases*" — medical evaluations are important in all patients

Medical Complications Resulting from Psychiatric Disorders

Schizophrenia
• Respiratory disorders and lung cancer from cigarette smoking
• Coronary artery disease due to poor diet, obesity, lack of exercise
• Dental caries from anticholinergic side-effects of medication
• Movement disorders can occur even without neuroleptic exposure

Mood Disorders
• Trauma from accidents or fights during manic episodes
• Infections from impaired immune function during depression
• Obesity from hyperphagia, carbohydrate craving during certain types of depressive episodes and antidepressant side effects

Anxiety Disorders
• Chronic anxiety can cause medical conditions in target organs — gastrointestinal and cardiac systems are most commonly affected

Bulimia Nervosa
• Electrolyte disturbances, dehydration, alkalosis
• Seizures related to electrolyte abnormalities
• Mallory-Weiss tears due to repeated vomiting
• Intestinal motility disturbances related to use of cathartics
• Parotid gland enlargement

Anorexia Nervosa
• The most worrisome complications are cardiac: arrhythmias, bradycardia, hypotension and congestive heart failure
• Reduced thyroid metabolism, leading to cold intolerance
• All blood cell counts can be decreased (pancytopenia)
• Kidney stones, osteoporosis
• Liver function tests become abnormal, amylase levels increase
• Amenorrhea; hypercortisolemia
• Delayed gastric emptying and bowel motility

Somatoform Disorders, Conversion Disorders, Malingering, Factitious Disorders
• Chronic complaints of illness can result in unnecessary investigations and therapeutic procedures (with their inherent risks)
• Such patients are also at risk for prescription medication abuse

Regional Brain Functions

Frontal Lobe — "LIMP"

Language — Broca's speech area
Intelligence, abstraction
Motor function
Personality

Temporal Lobe — "LAME"

Language — Wernicke's speech area
Affective component of speech — prosody
Memory
Emotion

Parietal Lobe — "VAST"

Visuospatial processing
Association areas — integration of sensory input
Symbolic recognition
Topographic sense

Occipital Lobe — "VIP"

Visual **I**ntergration area
Primary visual cortex

 **Memory Tidbits**

| retrograde amnesia | event | anterograde amnesia |

⬅ ▲ time ➡

Memory

Brain areas involved in memory:
- Verbal memory   dominant temporal lobe
- Visual memory   nondominant temporal lobe
- Registration   frontal & temporal lobes
- Short-term memory   hippocampus (consolidation & retrieval); temporal lobe (storage); medial dorsal thalamic nuclei (storage)
- Long-term memory   association cortex of temporal lobe (medial temporal region)

Structures involved in memory:
- Hippocampus — has connections to the thalamus and temporal lobe; part of the limbic system
- Amygdala — involved in the integration of memories and the recognition of faces; part of the limbic system
- Mamillary bodies — implicated in the pathology of Korsakoff's Syndrome; part of the hypothalamus
- Pulvinar — needed for memory retrieval; part of the thalamus

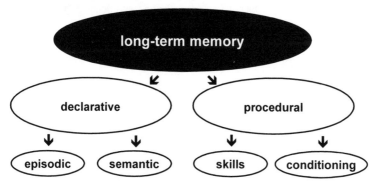

- **Declarative memory** is factual and directly accessible to consciousness. It is also called "knowing that" or "knowing what" memory. *Episodic memory* involves the recall of events and the context in which they occurred (where, when, etc.). *Semantic memory* refers to knowledge not remembered in a specific context.
- **Procedural memory** refers to acquired skills and habits. It is also called "knowing how" memory. This type of memory evolves after many trials, and remains largely intact in various forms of amnesia, unlike declarative memory.

Regional Brain Testing

Frontal Lobe

- Rapid sequential movements
- Complex motor behaviors
- Ability to repeat phrases with prosody
- Problem solving, judgment, concentration, orientation

Temporal Lobe

- Reading
- Writing
- Naming
- Gnosis — recognition of numbers and letters
- Comprehension of spoken language

Parietal Lobe

- Praxis
  - ideomotor — ability to carry out actions on command
  - ideational — ability to carry out acts in a logical sequence
  - constructional — ability to arrange shapes and copy diagrams
- Calculation
- Stereognosis
- Right-left and east-west orientation

Occipital Lobe

- Visual memory
- Pattern recognition

Cognitive Functioning Parameters

- Level of Consciousness/Alertness
- Orientation
- Attention & Concentration
- Memory — Registration (Immediate, Recent, Remote)
- Intelligence Estimation
- Knowledge Base/Fund of Information
- Capacity to Read and Write
- Abstraction/Concrete Thinking
- Visuospatial Ability

Regional Brain Dysfunction

Frontal Lobe

- Impaired complex motor behavior
- Inability to repeat phrases with **prosody**
- **Broca's Aphasia** (non-fluent)
- Impaired rapid sequential movements
- Impaired problem solving, judgment, concentration and orientation

Temporal Lobe

Unilateral Dominant
- Memory problems
- **Wernicke's Aphasia** (fluent)

Unilateral Non-dominant
- Impaired recognition of sounds
- Disorder of speech prosody

Bilateral
- Korsakoff's Syndrome
- Klüver-Bucy Syndrome⁺
- Language, memory and emotion are affected
    - Writing and naming (neologisms are made-up words)
    - Gnosis — recognition of numbers and letters
    - Comprehension of spoken language

⁺ hypersexuality, hyperorality, psychic blindness and placidity

Parietal Lobe

Dominant
- Gerstmann's Syndrome*
- Alexia with agraphia
- Astereognosis
- Language recognition
  and word memory impairment

Non-Dominant
- Disorders of spatial awareness
- Calculation problems
- Impairment of right-left, east-west
  orientation

* agraphia, acalculia, finger agnosia and left-right disorientation

Occipital Lobe

- Anton's Syndrome — cortical blindness and denial of blindness
- Balint's Syndrome — gaze paralysis & abnormal guidance of limbs
- Agnosia for faces and colors
- Alexia (inability to read)

Delirium

Delirium is not an illness, but a syndrome involving a disturbance of consciousness. Cognitive functions are globally impaired, with an inability to focus or sustain attention, and often with abnormalities of perception. The onset is usually rapid, with a fluctuating course.

Biological Features
• Common causes include CNS diseases, medical illnesses and substance intoxication or withdrawal
• Some patients have psychiatric conditions that predispose them to develop delirium, but these illnesses are not the primary cause
• **Acetylcholine** is thought to be the major neurotransmitter affected; the **reticular formation** regulates consciousness

Psychosocial Features
• Up to 15% of medical/surgical patients experience delirium
• Removal from familiar surroundings may hasten delirium

Mental Status Examination
• Disorientation with a fluctuating level of consciousness is seen
• Hallucinations and illusions in any sensory modality can occur
• Language impairment (incoherence or rambling) is present
• Memory and general cognitive functions are grossly impaired
• The **MMSE** is useful to gauge impairment and monitor progress

Biological Treatment
• The precipitating factor for the delirium should be identified and corrected as soon as possible (sepsis, drug interactions, etc.)
• Non-essential medications should be discontinued, and biochemical and hematologic abnormalities corrected
• Patients may need restraints to prevent accidental injuries
• Antipsychotic medication (usually **haloperidol** due to its safety profile) is indicated to diminish perceptual aberrations

Psychosocial Treatment
• Placement near nursing stations, illumination of rooms and constant reorientation can be helpful during lucid moments
• Familiar faces, voices and belongings are comforting

Prognosis
• Overall prognosis is very poor; the 3-month mortality is as high as 33%; 1-year mortality 50%; duration of delirium is a key factor

Delirium

"DELIRIUM"

Disoriented — time (most common) > place > person (least common)
Emotionally labile
Level of consciousness is impaired and fluctuates
Irrelevant stimuli distract the patient's attention
Rapid onset (hours to days)
Integration of perceptions is lost
Utterances — incoherent speech
Memory is impaired (especially immediate and recent recall)

 Delirium Tidbits

• Perceptual disturbances, sleep-wake cycle abnormalities and incoherent speech help distinguish delirium from dementia

• Delirious patients frequently sleep poorly and experience a reversal of sleep patterns; a phenomenon known as **sundowning** may occur — this is an exacerbation of symptoms due to a less stimulating environment (less light, fewer sounds and people around, etc.)

• The majority of cases of delirium are due to medical conditions existing outside the central nervous system

• The hallucinations and delusions expressed in delirium are often of psychodynamic relevance; try and get as much detail as possible, as it may be helpful after recovery

• Once treated effectively, delirium can remit quickly

• Anticholinergic medications are a common cause of delirium; unfortunately, many psychiatric medications are anticholinergic, particularly drugs used to treat extrapyramidal symptoms (known as **anticholinergic agents**) ➔ if anticholinergic toxicity is suspected, **physostigmine** (a reversible inhibitor of acetylcholinesterase which crosses the blood-brain barrier) can be administered IV as both an investigative and therapeutic agent; it is also used in TCA overdoses

• Many neurologic symptoms can be seen during delirium, e.g. incontinence, tremor, gait abnormalities, asterixis

Dementia of the Alzheimer's Type

Dementia is a continual and irreversible decline in cognitive function after the brain has matured. It is a syndrome characterized by intellectual impairment manifested in altered perception, mentation and behavior. Dementia of the Alzheimer's Type (DAT) is the most common form, and involves primarily an impairment of memory, with at least one other cognitive deficit.

Biological Features
• DAT is diagnosed conclusively at autopsy; characteristic findings include plaques, tangles, astrocytic gliosis and loss of neurons
• DAT occurs in a parietal-temporal lobe distribution
• Genetic factors are becoming better established; the dementia in **Down's Syndrome** shares similar pathological findings
• A deficit of cholinergic transmission is hypothesized

Psychosocial Features
• 5% of patients over 65, and 25% of those over 85 have dementia
• Patients can develop a support network that covers their deficits
• A **catastrophic reaction** can result when patients become aware of their deficits in stressful situations
• **Sundowning** also occurs in DAT (see the section on Delirium)

Mental Status Examination
• Memory and general cognitive functions are the most impaired
• The **MMSE** is useful to gauge impairment and monitor progress

Biological Treatment
• **Donepezil (Aricept)** is a reversible cholinesterase inhibitor which may improve symptoms in mild to moderate dementia
• **Antidepressants**, **antipsychotics** and **anxiolytics** can be used for target symptoms; patients with dementia are very sensitive both to the direct and side effects of medication

Psychosocial Treatment
• Supportive treatment and education are beneficial; community organizations are helpful; optimizing the environment also helps

Prognosis
• Overall survival rate is about 8 years; a younger age of onset or family history often indicates a more rapid decline

Dementia of the Alzheimer's Type

"DEAR GRAMPA"

Decline in social or occupational functioning
Executive functioning declines
Apraxia — motor activities are impaired
Rule out — delirium, substance use and general medical conditions

Gradual onset and continual decline
Runs in families — ask about **R**elatives
Aphasia — language impairment
Memory impairment
Personality changes can occur (disinhibition, exaggerated traits)
Agnosia — failure to recognize objects

Dementia Tidbits

• DAT and vascular dementias account for over 75% of cases; other common causes are neurodegenerative, infectious, traumatic, metabolic disorders, and dementia due to movement disorders

• Personality changes in DAT can become marked

• Psychotic symptoms (usually paranoid delusions) can occur

• An important psychiatric condition to exclude is depression; the poor cognitive performance is called **pseudodementia**

• Substance Abuse, particularly with solvents, inhalants or alcohol can cause dementia; heavy metal poisoning and organophosphate insecticides are important occupational causes of dementia

• **Benign senescent forgetfulness** involves trouble with word-finding, but does not cause social or occupational impairment

• Medications commonly used to treat aggression in dementia are: **propranolol**, **trazodone**, **buspirone** and **antipsychotics**

• The ability to focus and sustain attention is most impaired in delirium, it is less affected in dementia or depression

• In mental retardation, a normal level of intelligence does not develop, which is a key distinguishing feature from dementia

Substance-Related Disorders

Substance-Related Disorders have an incredible impact on society, with up to 1 in 8 people having a substance-related disorder. The DSM-IV defines conditions based on **intoxication** and **withdrawal** for each drug of abuse. Additionally, two use-related disorders are recognized, **Substance Abuse** and **Substance Dependence**.

Substances can induce almost any psychiatric illness, with the substance-induced variant being indistinguishable from the naturally-occurring disorder. **Dual Diagnosis** is a term used to denote the **comorbidity** of two or more psychiatric conditions.
In practice, this often refers to a major clinical syndrome (e.g. schizophrenia) complicated by a substance-related disorder.

Substance use impedes a proper diagnostic assessment. As a result, a period of abstinence is necessary to determine whether the etiology is substance related. Substance use also reduces the efficacy of treatment interventions, and obscures an evaluation of treatment response. In general, it is a poor prognostic indicator.

Drugs of Abuse

"COCAINE CHOPS"

Cocaine

Opioids

Cannabis

Amphetamines

Inhalants & Solvents

Nicotine

Ethanol & Non-beverage alcohol

Caffeine

Hallucinogens

Other

PCP — phencyclidine

Sedative-hypnotics

Substance Abuse

"HELP"

Hazardous circumstances do not deter substance use
Evasion of obligations due to substance use
Legal difficulties caused by use of substance
Problems (social and interpersonal) develop due to use

Substance Dependence

"ROLAID PUPILS"

Relief of withdrawal symptoms with a substance (withdrawal criterion #2)
Occupational/social/recreational activities are given up or reduced
Larger amounts are taken than intended
Awareness of problems related to substance use
Increased amounts are needed for same effect (tolerance criterion #1)
Diminished effect with use of the same amount (tolerance criterion #2)

Persistent desire to cut down or control use
Unsuccessful efforts to cut down or control use
Personal problems (social and interpersonal) due to use
Investment of time in substance-related activity is considerable
Longer duration of use than initially intended
Symptoms of withdrawal occur (withdrawal criterion #1)

Substance Use Tidbits

• The signs and symptoms of dependence or abuse must be present within the same 12-month period to make the diagnosis
• Dependence is a more serious condition than abuse; if the criteria for dependence have been met, abuse is not diagnosed
• Almost any psychiatric illness can be caused or mimicked by substance use — *ask all patients about their use of substances*

Ethanol Withdrawal

"PINT OF ASA"

Perceptual disturbances — hallucinations or illusions

Insomnia, Irritability

Nausea and/or vomiting

Tremor — usually seen in the hands

Onset is from hours to 3 days after the last consumption

Flushing of the face seen

Autonomic hyperactivity — heart rate, blood pressure, temperature

Seizures — grand mal (tonic-clonic)

Agitation

 Alcohol Withdrawal Tidbits

• Alcohol withdrawal is more likely to occur with heavy, prolonged consumption in the presence of malnourishment and coexisting physical ailments

• Patients with seizures that persist beyond 48 hours should be investigated for other conditions (metabolic, neurologic, etc.)

• Administer **thiamine (vitamin B₁)** prior to giving food or glucose (it is a cofactor in carbohydrate metabolism); **Wernicke-Korsakoff Syndrome** (ataxia, confusion, ophthalmoplegia) can be precipitated by giving glucose first

• Long-acting benzodiazepines are the mainstay of treatment for alcohol withdrawal (**chlorazepate, chlordiazepoxide, diazepam**); multivitamins and magnesium are often added

• If patients have severe liver disease, use **lorazepam, oxazepam** or **temazepam (LOT)** to avoid accumulation of active metabolites

• **Delirium tremens** (alcohol withdrawal delirium) is a complication of alcohol withdrawal; the onset is 1 to 3 days after cessation of drinking; mortality rates can be as high as 20%

• Patients with alcohol use disorders commonly fall or get into physical fights — consider a **subdural hematoma**

• Withdrawal seizures do not generally require prophylaxis or continuation of treatment after the withdrawal has passed

Opioid Withdrawal

"A MANY PAIN DEAL"

Antagonist precipitates withdrawal *

Mood is dysphoric
Aches in muscles and bones
Nausea and/or vomiting
Yawning

Piloerection — "gooseflesh" (the origin of the term "cold turkey")
Agonist removes withdrawal symptoms
Insomnia
Not life threatening

Diarrhea
Elevated temperature
Abdominal cramps
Lacrimation and rhinorrhea

 Opioid Tidbits

* Opioid antagonists (**naloxone, naltrexone**) can block the euphoric effects that accompany morphine, heroin, demerol, etc.

• Avoid using **demerol (meperidine)** with MAOIs

• Constipation and miosis do not diminish as tolerance develops

• Withdrawal from short-acting opioids can occur as soon as 6 hours, and up to 3 days for longer-acting opioids

• Any opioid can reverse withdrawal symptoms

• In practice, **methadone** and **LAMM** are used to treat withdrawal symptoms — they are synthetic opioids that can be taken orally and have a long duration of action with a minimal degree of euphoria

• **Methadone Maintenance Programs** defer the withdrawal until patients are better prepared; these programs also reduce the use of needles, a major factor in the spread of HIV, Hepatitis B and other intravenously-transmitted infections

Schizophrenia/Schizophreniform Dis.

The term schizophrenia refers to the *schism* between thought, feelings and behavior in affected patients; it is characterized by:
• at least 1 month of **positive symptoms** (hallucinations, delusions, disorganized speech and behavioral changes)
• a 6-month period of continuous disturbance involving **deficit** or **negative symptoms** (see p. 50) and which may include positive symptoms in a full-scale or attenuated form

Biological Features
• Genetic Risk — MZ twins 40%; both parents 25%; one parent 15%; DZ twins/one sibling 10%; general risk 1%
• Structural brain changes and neurochemical, neurophysiological and endocrine abnormalities have been found on a consistent basis

Psychosocial Features
• The lifetime prevalence is approximately 1% of the population
• There is currently no evidence to implicate psychosocial causes in the etiology of schizophrenia
• Family and interpersonal factors have a significant impact on the course of the illness: **schisms** (family divisions), **skews** (power imbalances), **double bind** situations and **expressed emotion (EE)**, defined as being critical, hostile, or overinvolved with patients

Biological Treatment
• First episode psychosis should be investigated and managed on an inpatient basis; it is crucial to rule out substance use and general medical conditions that can cause psychosis
• Antipsychotic medication is the cornerstone of treatment
• Traditional antipsychotic medications work well for positive symptoms but are less effective for negative symptoms

Psychosocial Treatment
• Community care involves a **case manager**, vocational rehabilitation, social skills training and ongoing supportive therapy
• Family education is important to lower expressed emotion (**EE**)
• Housing in a group home or residence may need to be arranged

Prognosis
• Overall, the prognosis remains discouraging: only 25% lead relatively normal lives; over 50% need repeated hospitalizations

Schizophrenia/Schizophreniform Dis.

"HALDOL BENDER"

Hallucinations — most common type are auditory

Areas of function are impaired (social, occupational, etc.)

Length of the disturbance is 6 months or longer

Disorganized speech

Organic (general medical) causes have been excluded

Loosening of associations — a disorder of **thought form**

Behavioral changes — disorganized or catatonic behaviors

Exclude — mood disorders (with psychotic features), Schizoaffective Disorder

Negative symptoms (see p. 50)

Delusions — usually bizarre in content (occurrence is impossible)

Early (pervasive developmental) disorders not present

Recreational drug use excluded — e.g. amphetamines & cocaine

 Schizophrenia Tidbits

• **Schizophreniform Disorder** shares most of the criteria with
Schizophrenia except:
• the duration is at least 1 month and less than 6 months
• the level of functioning is not necessarily disrupted to the same degree

• **Positive symptoms** respond better to antipsychotics than
negative symptoms (which predominate with time — see p. 50)
• Paranoid schizophrenia tends to have a later onset and milder
course than other forms; Paranoid, Schizotypal and Schizoid
Personality Disorders are in the **schizophrenic spectrum** (p. 49)
• Good prognostic indicators are:
    • family history of mood disorders; older age of onset
    • psychotic symptoms shortly after psychosocial decline
    • confusion or perplexity when psychotic
    • good level of adjustment prior to the onset of symptoms
    • compliance with all types of treatment
    • avoidance of recreational drug use
    • no suicidal ideation or attempts at self-harm
    • female gender

Schizoaffective Disorder

Schizoaffective Disorder is listed as an "other psychotic disorder" in the DSM-IV. As the name implies, both psychotic and mood symptoms are present. The DSM-IV changed "affective disorders" to "mood disorders," however, the name of this condition was not changed to Schizomood Disorder — maybe because it sounds funny. Diagnosing this condition involves three parts:

Part 1

'A' Criteria for Schizophrenia

• delusions
• hallucinations
• disorganized speech
• behavioral changes
• negative symptoms

are present at the same time as a symptoms meeting the criteria for a mood disturbance (depressed, manic or mixed mood state)

Part 2

Psychotic Component

• delusions, or
• hallucinations are present for at least 2 weeks without prominent mood symptoms

Part 3

Mood Component

• depression, or
• mania, or a
• mixed episode is present for a substantial period of the total illness

 Schizoaffective Tidbits

• Considerable debate exists as to whether this is primarily a schizophrenic disorder, a mood disorder (bipolar type), a hybrid of both, or a distinct disorder
• Schizoaffective disorder has a prognosis intermediate between schizophrenia and mood disorders; patients with the bipolar subtype tend to fare better than those with the depressive subtype
• In general, patients require continual treatment for their mood symptoms and intermittent treatment for psychotic symptoms
• The criteria were constructed to avoid diagnosing mood disorders with psychotic features as Schizoaffective Disorder

The Schizophrenic Spectrum

Schizotypal PD*

Paranoid PD*

Schizoid PD*

Increasing Severity

Schizo-affective Disorder

Delusional Disorder

Psychotic Disorder NOS°

° NOS: Not Otherwise Specified

Paranoid Schizophrenia

Schizo-phrenia

Schizoaffective
• combination of mood and schizophrenic symptoms

Schizophreniform
• lesser in time course and severity than schizophrenia

Schizophrenia

Positive Symptoms	Negative Symptoms

Schizotypal PD*

Schizoid PD*

* PD: Personality Disorder

Negative Symptoms

Many clinicians divide the signs and symptoms of schizophrenia into **positive** and **negative symptoms,** also referred to as Type I and Type II schizophrenia, respectively. One way to conceptualize this distinction is that positive symptoms are *added* to the picture, negative ones are *deficits* in the clinical presentation. **Positive symptoms are: hallucinations, delusions, formal thought disorders** and **bizarre** or **disorganized behavior.**

Part of developing skills as an interviewer is to not only pay attention to what *is* being said or done, but also to what *is not* being said or done. In many ways, negative symptoms contribute more to the disability suffered in schizophrenia than do the positive symptoms. Negative symptoms have a slow, insidious onset, but impact on the patient's ability to work, live independently and stay in relationships.

"NEGATIVE TRACK"

Negligible response to conventional antipsychotics

Eye contact is decreased

Grooming & hygiene decline

Affective responses become flat

Thought blocking

Inattentiveness

Volition is diminished

Expressive gestures decrease

Time — increases the number of negative symptoms

Recreational interests diminish; **R**elationships decrease

A's — see below for 5 A's

Content of speech diminishes (poverty of thought)

Knowledge — cognitive deficits increase

aPathy/Avolition aLogia Affective Flattening aNhedonia/Asociality aTtentional impairment	**PLANT** mnemonic for the five **A**'s from the Scale for the Assessment of Negative Symptoms (SANS) provided by: **Dr. David Wagner** **Indiana University**

Negative Symptom Tidbits

The distinction between negative and positive symptoms is important for several reasons:

• When Kraepelin and Bleuler first described schizophrenia, they made distinctions between *fundamental* (positive) and *accessory* (negative) symptoms. By the way, Bleuler suggested the term schizophrenia in 1911 to refer to a splitting of the mind. Prior to this, Kraepelin called it **dementia praecox**.

• Negative symptoms are not usually treated effectively by traditional antipsychotic medication, whereas positive symptoms generally do respond. Newer antipsychotics (clozapine, olanzapine) appear to treat negative symptoms much more effectively.

• Of the five "A" criteria for schizophrenia, only one includes negative symptoms; the DSM-IV requires six months of **prodromal** or **residual symptoms**, which may consist largely or entirely of negative symptoms.

• Negative symptoms tend to become more prominent with time and are significantly disabling to patients. Statistically, those with primarily negative symptoms are unmarried males with an earlier onset, poorer course, and higher incidence of other behavioral abnormalities.

Dr. Nancy Andreason* developed standardized scales to more fully assess the presence of positive and negative symptoms. The scale for positive symptoms is called the **SAPS** (Scale for the Assessment of Positive Symptoms). The other is the **SANS** (Scale for the Assessment of Negative Symptoms; for those who appreciate puns, *sans* in French means "without"). The major headings in this scale are in the PLANT mnemonic on the previous page.

* The scales are available in major texts or from:
Dr. Nancy Andreason
Department of Psychiatry
College of Medicine
University of Iowa
Iowa City, IA
USA 52242

Catatonia

Catatonia is a term applied to a diverse number of postural and movement disturbances. The motor disorders can include both increased and decreased levels of activity. The term catatonia was developed by Kahlbaum and initially was a diagnostic entity on its own. If Kahlbaum had been a dog person, he would have called it *dogatonia*.

In the DSM-IV, catatonia is diagnosable in three forms:
• a subtype of schizophrenia
• a specifier for a mood episode
• due to a general medical condition

Catatonia is also found in:
• **Periodic catatonia**, a rare variant involving an alteration of thyroid function and nitrogen balance
• Neurologic illnesses that involve the basal ganglia, frontal lobes, limbic system and extrapyramidal pathways
• Syphilis and viral encephalopathies
• Head trauma, arteriovenous malformations, etc.
• Toxic states (e.g. alcoholism, fluoride toxicity)
• Metabolic conditions (e.g. hypoglycemia, hyperparathyroidism)

This mnemonic incorporating the DSM-IV criteria for catatonia is:

"WRENCHES"

Weird (peculiar) movements

Rigidity

Echopraxia — copying the body movements of others

Negativism — automatic opposition to all requests

Catalepsy (waxy flexibility)

High level of motor activity

Echolalia — repeating the words of others

Stupor — immobility

Catatonia Tidbits

Each of the letters in "**WRENCHES**" is explained in greater detail —

• Weird (peculiar) voluntary movements given as examples in the DSM-IV include: **inappropriate** or **bizarre postures, stereo-typed movements, mannerisms**, and **grimacing**.

• Rigidity, which can present in the following ways:
   Lead pipe: resistance to movement in all directions
   Cogwheel: a stop-and-go pattern, as seen in Parkinsonism
   Clasp Knife: resistance to a certain point, then giving way
Extreme rigidity can lead to muscle breakdown, acute renal failure, and in some cases, death (known as **lethal catatonia**).

• **Echopraxia** is the involuntary repetition of the movements of others (mimicry would be voluntary).

• **Negativism** refers to the automatic refusal to cooperate. Simple requests are strongly opposed for no obvious reason, even in cases where patients would benefit from participation (e.g. taking off a warm coat when inside). Patients typically either refuse, or do the exact opposite of what is asked of them.

• **Catalepsy (waxy flexibility, flexibilitas cerea)** is a phenomenon whereby patients can be moved into new postures or positions, and will stay this way for periods of thirty seconds or more.

• High level of motor activity, also called **catatonic excitement**, is an episode of hyperactive behavior consisting of a high-energy "running amok" that ends when the patient collapses in exhaustion or when treatment is initiated.

• **Echolalia** is the involuntary repetition of words, such as greetings, statements and questions, without patients being able to express their own thoughts. Again, this differs from mimicry in that patients don't do this of their own volition.

• **Stupor** is probably the most commonly known catatonic behavior. Patients can show a decrease in movement to the point of being mute and akinetic. They may also have a reduced awareness of their environment. A stupor can last for a prolonged time, and even lead to the point where an intervention is necessary for nutritional or hygienic reasons. An episode can end abruptly with a sudden outburst or impulsive act that is not in response to external stimuli.

Delusional Disorder

A delusion is a fixed, false belief out of keeping with cultural norms and the person's level of intelligence. Delusions are based on mistaken inferences about the environment and are not amenable to modification by reasoning. Delusional Disorder (DD) is listed as an "other psychotic disorder." The delusions are non-bizarre in nature, meaning the idea expressed is *possible*, even if it is not *probable*.

Biological Features:
• Disease processes affecting the **basal ganglia** and **limbic system** can produce complex delusions
• Physical impairment and disabilities, especially with sensory deficits, can induce persecutory thoughts

Psychosocial Features
• DD is a rare disorder, with a reported prevalence of 0.03% (schizophrenia is 30 times more common)
• Patients with DD often have very low self-esteem, fostered by an isolated environment, sadistic treatment or unreliable caretakers
• The main ego defense in paranoia is **projection** (attributing unacceptable inner experiences to others); other major defenses used are **denial** and **reaction formation**

Biological Treatment
• Delusional patients often resist taking medication
• Many **positive symptoms** are successfully treated with antipsychotics, but delusions typically have a poor response
• Some reports indicate **pimozide** may be useful for somatic delusions; **serotonergic antidepressants** have also been used
• If antipsychotics are effective, low doses are often sufficient

Psychosocial Treatment
• A wide range of psychotherapies can be used; therapy focuses on social integration instead of reducing delusional thinking
• Avoid both confronting or colluding with delusions
• Delusions often contain a "kernel" of truth

Prognosis
• The prognosis for DD is generally favorable; only about 25% of patients have no improvement in their symptoms
• 25% of patients are later rediagnosed with another condition

Delusional Disorder

"NO FAME"

Non-bizarre delusions (e.g. improbable, not impossible)
One-month minimum duration

Functioning is not markedly impaired
A — 'A' criteria of schizophrenia are not met (see p. 48)
Mood episodes are brief compared to duration of illness
Exclusion of substance-related and general medical conditions

"J-PEGS"   Jealous Type (Othello Syndrome)
                  Persecutory Type
                  Erotomanic Type (de Clérambault Syndrome)
                  Grandiose Type
                  Somatic Type

 Delusional Tidbits

• Delusional Disorder was previously called "Paranoid Disorder;" the name was changed to include other delusions where persecution is not the central theme
• Thoughts that are of less than delusional intensity are called **overvalued ideas**
• Kurt Schneider listed findings of particular value in diagnosing schizophrenia and called these **first-rank symptoms**. Of eleven first-rank symptoms, eight involve delusions that cause patients to feel under the control of external forces and respond passively, also called **delusions of passivity** or **passivity experiences**.

• **Thought Broadcasting** — patients experience their thoughts as being automatically broadcast to others (as if by television or radio)
• **Thought Insertion** — thoughts are inserted from an outside source
• **Thought Withdrawal** — thoughts are removed before being expressed
• **Insertion of Somatic Passivity** — submission to an external force
• **Insertion of Feelings** — "made" or forced feelings
• **Insertion of Impulses** — submission to an impulse
• **Insertion of an Outside Will** — passivity of volition
• **Delusional Perception** — the attribution of false (delusional) meanings to ordinary events

Delusional Tidbits

Despite their great variety, delusions fall into a set number of themes. As indicated below, delusions often relate to early developmental needs, struggles and milestones. Common themes involve one's body, nonexistence, one's self and the outside world. Delusions are given the suffix "mania" to denote an exaggerated interest in, or preference for something, but also implies a behavior or an action. Excessive ruminations are given the suffix "philia" indicating a disposition towards something. For example, *pyromania* refers to fire setting and *pyrophilia* refers to an excessive interest in fires.

Common delusional themes can be related to **Erickson's Life Cycle Stages**:

Stage	Central Issue	Theme of Delusion
• Basic Trust vs. Basic Mistrust	Safety	Paranoia
• Autonomy vs. Shame & Doubt	Bodily Functions	Somatization
• Initiative vs. Guilt	Achievement	Grandiosity
• Industry vs. Inferiority	Achievement	Grandiosity
• Identity vs. Role Diffusion	Love	Jealousy & Erotomania
• Intimacy vs. Isolation	Love	Jealousy & Erotomania

Culture-Bound Syndromes

A sampling of delusions from other cultures . . .
• **Brain Fag** — belief that the brain can suffer fatigue from overuse (Yes, this is what it is called. Some sources record this as "brain fog")
• **Koro** — belief that the penis or vulva will recede into the body and cause death (differentiate this from **kuru** which is a slow virus infection causing neurologic degeneration)
• **Rootwork/mal puesto** — belief that one can subject others, or be subjected, to hexes, spells or curses
• **Taijin kyofusho** — the belief that one's body or its parts and functions are offensive to others
• **Windigo** — delusion that one can be transformed into a giant monster that eats human flesh
• **Zar** — delusional possession by a spirit

Delusional Tidbits

Some Common Delusions

• **Animal Metamorphosis** — cat (galeanthropy), dog (cynanthropy), wolf (lycanthropy)
• **Cacodaemonomania** — poisoned by an evil spirit
• **Caesarmania** — delusion of grandiose ability (or inventing a garlic-laden salad)
• **Capgras' Syndrome** — an identical-looking impostor has replaced someone significant to the patient
• **Delusion of Reference** — ascribing personal meaning to common events; often involves the TV, newspapers or radio as having special messages just for the patient, but can include idiosyncratic associations (a bird flew by, therefore my car is low on oil)
• **Dorian Gray** — the person stays the same age while everyone else ages
• **Enosimania** — guilt, unworthiness for having committed some catastrophic deed
• **Folie à deux** — a delusion is transferred from a psychotic person to a recipient who accepts the belief
• **Folie induite** — transfer of a delusion to someone who is already psychotic; a delusion added to a pre-existing one
• **Fregoli's Syndrome** — a persecutor impersonates people the patient knows (the opposite of Capgras')
• **Incubus** — a demonic lover
• **Intermetamorphosis** — a familiar person (usually a persecutor) and a misidentified stranger share both physical and psychological attributes
• **Magical Thinking** — believing that an event will occur simply by wishing it so, as if by magic
• **Messianic** — being God (also called **theomania**)
• **Mignon** — being of royal lineage
• **Nihilism** — nonexistence; loss of organs, body or everything; damnation; sense of death or disintegration; also called **Cotard's Syndrome**
• **Phantom Boarder** — unwelcome delusional house guests
• **Poverty** — loss of all wealth and property
• **Reduplicative Paramnesia** — thinking that people, places or body parts have been duplicated (**heutoscopy** is also the delusion of having a double)
• **Wahnstimmung** (German) — delusions of persecution

Major Depressive Episode

A Major Depressive Episode (MDE) is one of two main mood disorders, the other being Bipolar Disorder. While transient diminution in mood is almost a universal human experience, an MDE is characterized by hopelessness, a sense of having lost control and loss of pleasure in addition to the depressed mood.

Biological Features
• Genetic factors are becoming increasingly evident; **adoption** and **twin studies** also support this finding (chromosomes 5, 11, 18, X)
• Serotonin and norepinephrine are the neurotransmitters involved in mood disorders; current antidepressant medications increase the availability of these compounds
• There are several biological changes in depression, e.g. sleep & circadian rhythm changes, endocrine & immune system changes

Psychosocial Features
• Lifetime prevalence for men is 15%; for women it is 25 to 30%
• Stressful events early in life may predispose to mood disorders
• Freud focused on the issue of **loss** in etiology of depression
• Frequently there are stressors (actual or symbolic) that occur prior to the onset of depression

Biological Treatment
• Antidepressants from different chemical classes appear to have similar efficacy, but vary widely in side effects
• Specific treatments may be indicated for subtypes of depression
• Onset of action takes at least 2 weeks and appears to be related to down-regulation of **post-synaptic noradrenergic beta receptors** and **type 2 serotonergic receptors**

Psychosocial Treatment
• Many effective psychotherapies exist for depression; cognitive, interpersonal and psychodynamic are the most common
• Combining psychotherapy with medication may produce the best outcome, though the issue is still open to debate

Prognosis
• The prognosis for MDE is generally favorable; at least 80% of patients fully recover; relapses are common with up to 25% occurring in the first year, 50% within 2 years and 75% within 5 years

Major Depressive Episode

"MASS FEE GAP FITS"

Mood is depressed for most of the day, almost everyday*
Activities are no longer of interest or pleasurable (**anhedonia**)*
Sleep changes — insomnia or hypersomnia*
Suicidal ideation*

Functioning is significantly impaired
Energy level is decreased*
Exclude — Mixed Episode and Bereavement

Guilt or worthlessness that is excessive or inappropriate*
Appetite changes (up or down); weight changes by 5% or more*
Psychomotor changes — agitation or retardation*

Five of nine symptoms needed (*marked with the* *)
Indecisiveness, poor concentration or diminished attention span*
Two-week minimum duration
Substance-Related Disorder excluded

 Depression Tidbits

• ECT is efficacious in Depression with Psychotic Features in up to 80% of patients (and works faster than medication); neuroleptics with antidepressants are effective in 60% of patients
• MAOIs may be more effective in treating depressive episodes with atypical features (p. 61) or when anxiety symptoms are prominent
• **Buproprion** (Wellbutrin — not available in Canada) is an antidepressant that increases dopamine levels
• **Hamilton, Zung & Beck** are rating scales for depression
• Beta-blockers, benzodiazepines and corticosteroids are the most common iatrogenic causes of depression
• Common augmentation strategies include: adding lithium, T_3, stimulants or neuroleptics to an antidepressant; use of combinations of TCAs, SSRIs and MAOIs are also used

Major Depressive Episode

"SAD IMAGES" [*]

Sleep changes — insomnia or hypersomnia
Appetite changes (up or down); weight changes by 5% or more
Depressed mood for most of the day, almost everyday

Indecisiveness, poor concentration and/or diminished attention span
Movements altered — psychomotor agitation or retardation
Activities are no longer of interest or pleasurable (**anhedonia**)
Guilt or worthlessness that is excessive or inappropriate
Energy level is decreased (fatigue)
Suicidal ideation

Depression Tidbits

[*] The above mnemonic contains only the nine DSM-IV criteria
• **Anomie** is a (real or imagined) lack of integration into society, leaving few social supports for the person
• **Apathy** is a "lack of feeling" characterized by diminished energy and interest in the environment; such patients are unemotional and listless; apathy has been described as a mood state and occurs with frontal lobe damage, schizophrenia, depression, and substance abuse (e.g. sedatives, marijuana, etc.)
• **Alexithymia** is the inability to sense and describe mood states; patients are "disconnected" from their feelings and describe them in terms of physical sensations or behaviors; this is seen in schizophrenia, posttraumatic stress disorder & somatoform disorders
• **Euthymia** is the word used to describe normal mood
• The criteria used to diagnose the dysphoric mood states of depression, cyclothymia & dysthymia are different
• There is no clear means of distinguishing sustained affect from reactive mood. Certain conditions (e.g. personality disorders, substance abuse) in which there is a good deal of variation in the moment-to-moment expression of emotion can occur comorbidly with mood disorders. To complicate matters, there is a variant of a bipolar mood disorder called a **mixed state** where manic and depressive symptoms occur simultaneously.

Melancholic Features Specifier
"PAGER MAD"

Psychomotor changes are marked (retardation or agitation)

Anorexia or weight loss

Guilt is excessive or inappropriate

Early morning awakening

Reactivity is lacking to stimuli that are usually pleasurable

Morning depression is regularly worse

Activities bring no pleasure (**anhedonia**)

Distinct quality of depressed mood

 Melancholic Features Tidbits

• Melancholic features are thought to indicate a type of depression that is likely to respond to medication

• A mood disturbance with these features has been referred to as **endogenous** (lacking an obvious precipitant), as opposed to a depression with obvious precipitants (called a **reactive depression**)

Atypical Features Specifier
"RAILS"

Reactivity of mood — changes with positive experiences

Appetite increases — **hyperphagia**

Interpersonal rejection sensitivity

Leaden paralysis — limbs feels as if they are made of lead

Sleep is increased — **hypersomnia**

 Atypical Features Tidbits

• The presence of atypical features may indicate a form of depression that may be preferentially responsive to MAOIs or SSRIs

• Atypical features may also indicate that the depressive episode is part of a bipolar mood disorder, and that the patient may in time develop manic or hypomanic episodes

Bipolar Mood Disorder

Bipolar Mood Disorder (BMD) refers to the presence of Manic Episodes and Major Depressive Episodes, and is also called **Manic-Depressive Illness**. Even if patients suffer only manic episodes, however, this diagnosis still applies. BMD usually starts with an episode of depression, and has an average age of onset 10 years earlier (about 30 years) than MDE (about 40 years)

Biological Features
• Genetic correlates are stronger for BMD than for MDE; over 90% of patients have a relative with a mood disorder
• **Kindling** is the repeated sub-threshold stimulation of a nerve cell that eventually causes it to fire; temporal lobe kindling may be a factor in the etiology of the mood changes seen in BMD
• Neuroimaging has revealed ventricular enlargement more consistently in BMD than in depression

Psychosocial Features
• BMD has a lifetime prevalence of 1% with an equal sex ratio
• BMD occurs more frequently in higher socio-economic classes
• BMD has been correlated with enhanced creativity

Biological Treatment
• Mood stabilizers (**lithium, carbamazepine, valproic acid**) are the mainstay of treatment for BMD
• Management of an acute manic episode requires a neuroleptic or benzodiazepine (usually **clonazepam**)
• Second-line medication for BMD includes **clozapine, verapamil** (a calcium channel blocker), and **clonidine** (an α_2 agonist)

Psychosocial Treatment
• During depressive phases, psychotherapy can be helpful
• Education for patients and families is crucial; principal teaching points involve the course of the illness, the benefits of compliance, and warning signs of an impending manic or depressive episode

Prognosis
• The prognosis for BMD is less favorable than for MDE
 • 50% of patients have another manic episode within 2 years
 • only 10% of patients are free from future manic episodes
 • 30% of bipolar patients have chronic symptoms that impair their ability

Manic/Hypomanic Episode
"FAST DIGGERS"

Functioning is severely impaired
Activities pursued with the potential for painful consequences*
Substance-Related Disorders excluded
Talkative — both *rate* and *amount* of speech are increased*

Distractibility*
Ideas racing (**flight of ideas**)*
Grandiose; inflated self-esteem*
Goal-directed activity is increased*
Elevated or Expansive mood (can also be irritable)
Rule out General Medical Conditions
Sleep requirement is lessened*

 Bipolar Tidbits

• With *irritable* mood, 4/7 criteria are required; with an *elevated* or *expansive* mood, 3/7 are required to make this diagnosis (the DSM-IV criteria are marked with an *)
• A Hypomanic Episode differs from Mania in the following ways:
  • The duration of symptoms only needs to be present for 4 days
  • The ability to function in important roles is not impaired
  • Hospitalization is not required and there are no psychotic symptoms
• A Course Specifier for BMD is called **Rapid Cycling**:
  • This involves 4 or more episodes of mood disturbance within 1 year
  • A cycle is the recovery (full or partial) from the most current mood disturbance (i.e. euthymic mood for at least two months), or a switch to the opposite mood polarity
  • Cycling can be triggered by antidepressants and thyroid dysfunction
  • This subtype has a poor response to lithium
• **Seasonal Pattern** & **Postpartum Onset** are course specifiers
• Ask about manic/hypomanic symptoms in depressed patients
• Manic Episodes can be caused by: multiple sclerosis, head injuries, Huntington's disease, epilepsy and corticosteroid use
• Elevated mood states occur in schizophrenia (disorganized type), substance abuse (usually with stimulants), dementia and delirium

Dysthymic Disorder

"HE TAILS"

Hopelessness
Esteem is decreased

Two-year duration (minimum)
Appetite changes (up or down)
Indecisiveness
Lethargy — Low energy
Sleep changes (increased or decreased)

Dysthymic Disorder (DD) (dysthymic means "ill humored") is a chronic mood disturbance. DD lacks the severity and episodic nature of a Major Depressive Episode. This diagnosis is common (3% prevalence) and can be a feature of other disorders, sharing a particular overlap with the Borderline Personality Disorder. One third of patients develop a more serious mood disorder. MAOIs, SSRIs and cognitive therapy are effective treatment modalities.

Cyclothymic Disorder

Cyclothymic Disorder (CD) is characterized by the presence of mood fluctuations that do not reach manic highs or major depressive lows. At one point it was considered a personality disorder. The current concept of CD overlaps with the Borderline Personality Disorder and other Cluster B personalities. CD is a chronic disorder that must be present over at least two years. The mood fluctuation can occur over the course of hours. Episodes with mixed symptoms are also common. One third of patients eventually develop a more serious mood disorder, often a Bipolar II Disorder. Mood stabilizers are indicated in the same doses that would be used in Bipolar Disorders (use antidepressants cautiously, particularly tricyclics).

Mood Disorder Patterns

Manic
Hypomanic
Euthymic
Depressive Symptoms
Major Depression

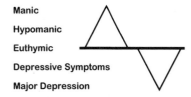

Bipolar Disorder Type I

• Manic and Depressive Episodes
• Depressive Episodes in some patients are brief or nonexistent
• No separate diagnostic category exists for Unipolar Mania

Manic
Hypomanic
Euthymic
Depressive Symptoms
Major Depression

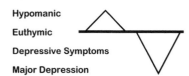

Bipolar Disorder Type II

• Hypomania with Major Depressive Episodes; the implications of the distinction from Bipolar Type I are still being investigated

Manic
Hypomanic
Euthymic
Depressive Sx.
Major Depression

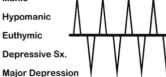

Rapid Cycling Type

• 4 or more episodes of Mania, Hypomania, Mixed, or MDE in 1 year
• Recovery for 2 months between episodes, or a switch to a mood episode of opposite polarity

Manic
Hypomanic
Euthymic
Depressive Sx.
Major Depression

Cyclothymic Disorder

• Depressive symptoms do not necessarily meet the criteria for a Dysthymic Disorder and are not as severe as an MDE; highs can be hypomanic in intensity

Manic
Hypomanic
Euthymic
Depressive Sx.
Major Depression

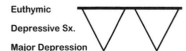

Major Depressive Episode

• Depressive symptoms are of significant duration & severity; usual course is a full recovery, but may have future episodes (the example here shows **recurrent episodes**)

Manic
Hypomanic
Euthymic
Depressive Sx.
Major Depression

Dysthymic Disorder

• Depressive symptoms are not severe enough for an MDE
• Some patients do develop a coexisting MDE; this is then called a **Double Depression**

Mood Disorder Tidbits

• Mood is evaluated according to the following parameters:
  • Quality   • Reactivity • Intensity   • Stability

• **Quality** of mood is the patient's reported emotional state. The DSM-IV includes the following mood types:
  • Depressed • Euphoric   • Anxious   • Angry/Irritable

• **Reactivity** is the degree to which mood is altered by external factors. Mood can be shifted by events, the environment or interactions with others. Manic patients often escalate in mood with stimulation. Depressed patients may feel worse in the morning and have their spirits lift as the day progresses. Similarly, anxious or angry patients have a waxing and waning of their mood under certain conditions.

• **Intensity** refers to the degree to which the mood is expressed. Like affect, mood has depth, amount or amplitude. Two patients can experience depressed mood with a similarly flat affect and restricted range of emotional expression. One patient may appear lethargic, withdrawn and show little interest in the interview. The other patient may have problems with concentration, lowered self-esteem and be able to convey the degree to which this episode has interfered with his or her life. The difference between these patients is the depth or intensity of their mood states.

• **Stability** or duration describes the length of time the mood disturbance exists without significant variation. Mood disorders are required to have a specific time course:

Major Depressive Episode	2 weeks
Manic Episode	1 week
Dysthymic Disorder	2 years
Cyclothymia	2 years

Mood Disorder Tidbits

• The terms **mood-congruent** and **mood-incongruent** are applied to delusions and hallucinations (psychotic features) that occur with mood disorders.

• The themes of depression are guilt, worthlessness, death, failure, hopelessness, punishment, illness, etc. If the content of delusions in depressed patients forms along these lines, the term *mood-congruent* is applied.

• In manic episodes, mood-congruent delusions follow the themes of power, brilliance, wealth, longevity, achievement, special relationships or connections, knowledge, etc.

• Manic patients with delusions of nihilism, poverty or inadequacy have *mood-incongruent delusions*, as do depressed patients with delusions of grandeur, omnipotence or relationships to famous people. Mood-incongruent delusions are a poor prognostic sign and may indicate the presence of a schizoaffective or schizophreniform disorder.

• Depressed mood is often accompanied by changes in:
  • Appearance (decline in self-care)
  • Behavior (few spontaneous movements)
  • Speech (speak softly, have little to say, etc.)
  • Affect (restricted range, variable intensity)
  • Thought content (morbid themes)
  • Thought form (increased latency of responses)
  • Diminished cognitive functioning

• Euphoric mood often occurs with changes in:
  • Appearance (unusual or bizarre changes)
  • Behavior (rapid, continual movements)
  • Speech (speak loudly, have a great deal to say, etc.)
  • Affect (expanded range, labile, intense)
  • Thought content (grandiose themes)
  • Thought form (flight of ideas, pressure of speech)
  • Cognitive functions may be enhanced (creativity or word associations) or diminished because of distractibility

• There are a large number of '**d**' words that describe depression:
(amaze your friends!) down, dejected, despondent, demoralized, dysphoric, despairing, dour, dispirited, drained, doleful, downcast, down in the dumps, desperate, defeated, dreary, disappointed, disillusioned, dissatisfied, disaffected, disconsolate & downhearted

• There are a large number of '**e**' words that describe mania:
energized, elevated, elated, entertaining, exalted, extreme, expansive, extraordinary, ecstatic, effervescent, excited, effusive & ebullient

Panic Attack/Panic Disorder

A **panic attack** consists of a discrete episode of intense discomfort involving neurologic, cardiovascular, gastrointestinal and psychic symptoms. Panic attacks occur in a variety of conditions and are not recognized as a distinct disorder in the DSM-IV. **Panic Disorder** consists of recurrent, unexpected panic attacks which are followed by one month of:
• continual concern about future attacks
• worry about the consequences of an attack
• significantly altered behavior

Biological Features
• Several substances can induce panic attacks: caffeine, inhalation of CO_2, infusion of lactate and **yohimbine** (an α_2 antagonist)
• Central noradrenergic and peripheral autonomic hyperactivity account for many of the somatic features of Panic Disorder
• Panic Disorder appears to have a distinct genetic component

Psychosocial Features
• The lifetime prevalence of panic attacks is 5%, and 2% for Panic Disorder; women appear twice as likely to be affected
• Panic attacks can be considered an adult form of **separation anxiety**; patients may have a history of this condition
• This disorder involves an exaggerated response to conditions that are misinterpreted as threatening (e.g. bodily sensations)
• Psychosocial stressors commonly precipitate panic attacks

Biological Treatment
• **TCAs, MAOIs, SSRIs** and **benzodiazepines** can all be effective
• **Beta-blockers** and **buspirone** are ineffective for this condition
• Panic attacks can be treated acutely with benzodiazepines

Psychosocial Treatment
• Cognitive-behavioral therapies can be at least as efficacious as somatic treatments; combining both may be the most effective
• **In vivo exposure** and **relaxation training** are also used

Prognosis
• This has a favorable outcome — 80% of patients are either symptom free or affected only mildly over time; **agoraphobia**, mood disorders or substance-related disorders worsen the prognosis — up to 50% of patients develop one of these conditions

Panic Attack/Panic Disorder

"THIS ISN'T FUN"

Trembling
Hot flushes
Increased heart rate
Sweating

Inspiration — intake of air feels obstructed, choking sensation
Smothering, **S**hortness of breath
Numbness or tingling in the limbs (**paresthesias**)
Tightness in the chest

Fear of: losing control, going crazy, or dying
Unreal sense of: self (**depersonalization**)
                        the environment (**derealization**)
Nausea or abdominal distress

 Panic Tidbits

• **Anticipatory anxiety** is the apprehensive expectation of another panic attack; this can become so pervasive that it is difficult to distinguish from Generalized Anxiety Disorder
• **Hyperthyroidism, pheochromocytoma** and **hypoglycemia** are common medical causes for panic attacks; **mitral valve prolapse** may be more prevalent in patients with Panic Disorder
• Typical situations that induce panic attacks are: driving a motor vehicle, crossing a bridge, and leaving one's neighborhood or city
• States of anxiety decrease blood flow to the frontal regions of the brain; some asymmetry of cerebral blood flow has been found in patients who suffer from panic attacks
• The presence of **mitral valve prolapse** (MVP) is not a significant factor in the treatment or prognosis of this disorder
• It is unusual for the onset of this disorder to occur after age 45
• Vertigo, parathyroid dysfunction, carcinoid syndrome and porphyria are rarer medical causes of panic attacks (see p. 143)

Phobic Disorders

A **phobia** is characterized by:
• a marked and persistent fear of an object or situation
• immediate symptoms of anxiety upon exposure to the object/situation
• avoidance of the object or situation

The DSM-IV lists two major categories of phobic disorders:
• **Social Phobia** (Social Anxiety Disorder)
• **Specific Phobia** (Subtypes are Animal, Natural Environment, Blood-Injection-Injury, Situational and Other — see p. 72)

Biological Features
• **Behavioral inhibition** is a temperamental factor that may predispose to phobic disorders
• Patients with phobias may have strong **vasovagal responses**
• Family studies provide some evidence for genetic transmission

Psychosocial Features
• Phobias affect up to 10% of the population
• Psychoanalytic and behavioral factors appear on p. 71
• **Displacement** and **symbolization** are the key ego defenses

Biological Treatment
• Specific phobias do not have a recommended treatment
• Social phobias respond more favorably to medication:
   • **Performance Anxiety** can be treated with **propranolol**
   • Generalized Social Phobia is often responsive to **phenelzine**

Psychosocial Treatment
• Specific and social phobias can be treated with cognitive-behavioral approaches involving **in vivo exposure, relaxation training, self-talk** and **self-hypnosis**
• Psychodynamic approaches treat Social Phobia as part of a larger character disturbance (e.g. Avoidant Personality Disorder);
• Psychodynamic psychotherapy seeks to discover the unconscious issues creating the phobia

Prognosis
• The prognosis for phobic disorders is generally favorable:
   • 80% of patients with specific phobias improve
   • Social Phobia tends to be lifelong with a waxing and waning course
   • comorbid conditions (depression, other anxiety disorders and substance-related disorders) are common and worsen the prognosis

Phobic Disorders

"FEARED"

Fear that is excessive and unreasonable

Exposure to the stimulus provokes anxiety

Avoids the phobic situation or object

Recognizes that the fear is excessive

Exclusion of other mental disorders (e.g. OCD, PTSD)

Distress is experienced in the feared situation

Phobic Disorder Tidbits

• **Learning theory** factors that are thought to be operative in the development of phobias are:

• **Classical conditioning**, which involves coupling a neutral stimulus with one that evokes a response, so that over time the neutral stimulus causes the same reaction (e.g. Pavlov's dogs salivating to the sound of a bell)

• **Operant conditioning**, in which learning occurs on a trial and error basis, with certain responses being reinforced with rewards or punishments

• Psychoanalytic theory proposes that unacceptable impulses (i.e. sexual or aggressive) arouse a conflict, causing anxiety, which then leads to the recruitment of an ego defense

Instinctual drive causing conflict
↓
Signal anxiety to the ego
↓
Use of repression as the primary defense
↓
Use of displacement or symbolization as secondary defenses
↓
Development of a phobia

• The phobic stimulus may have a connection with the source of the conflict (called **symbolization**), e.g. a fear of trains in a patient with **separation anxiety**

• Freud developed his theory of phobias through his work with **Little Hans**, a boy who displaced his Oedipal conflict from his father onto horses and developed a phobia of them (sort of a reverse Equus)

• **Counterphobic attitude** refers to the process whereby patients deny their phobic anxiety and seek feared objects or situations; this most commonly arises as a reaction to serious medical conditions (e.g. bungee jumping after recent surgery)

Phobic Disorder Tidbits

"ASP & BOAS" *

Animal type — e.g. killer chihuahuas or goldfish

Situational type — e.g. bridges, tunnels, flying, driving, etc.

People (social phobia) — e.g. public speaking

Blood/Injection — e.g. seeing blood or having procedures

Other — used when other categories simply won't do

Agoraphobia — avoidance of places where escape or getting help is difficult

Surroundings — elements in the natural environment such as storms, water, heights, etc.

* For those unfamiliar with reptilian suborder *ophidia*, an asp is a venomous snake (viper) and also makes an excellent *Scrabble* word; this mnemonic is helpful because snakes are a common phobia (even for Indiana Jones).

• **Agoraphobia** is a condition that deserves special mention. The word is derived from Greek and means "fear of the marketplace." The DSM-IV defines it as: *Anxiety about being in places or situations from which escape might be difficult (or embarrassing) or in which help may not be available in the event of having an unexpected or situationally predisposed panic attack or panic-like symptoms.*

Agoraphobia is a common phobia and the one that causes the greatest impairment of social and occupational functioning. Generally, patients who experience repeated panic attacks become "phobic" of the places where attacks occur, or where help or escape are difficult to arrange.

Patients with agoraphobia curtail their activities significantly. They make constant demands on friends and family members to accompany them on outings. Agoraphobia is frequently complicated by other phobias or obsessions. Additionally, depressive disorders and substance abuse often complicate the lives of agoraphobics.

Agoraphobia is coded in the DSM-IV in the following:
• Panic Disorder with/without Agoraphobia
• Agoraphobia Without History of Panic Disorder

Phobic Disorder Tidbits

Specific Phobias

New &
Unusual

• Anginaphobia — fear of narrowness
• Anuptophobia — fear of staying single
• Cherophobia — fear of good news
• Dementophobia — fear of insanity
• Ergophobia — fear of work
• Gelophobia — fear of laughing
• Genuphobia — fear of knees
• Glossophobia — fear of talking
• Gymnophobia — fear of naked bodies
• Herpetophobia — fear of lizards
• Iatrophobia — fear of doctors
• Kainophobia — fear of newness
• Kenophobia — fear of empty spaces
• Kleptophobia — fear of stealing
• Logophobia — fear of words
• Methyphobia — fear of alcohol
• Mnemonophobia — fear of memories
• Musophobia — fear of mice
• Myxophobia — fear of slime
• Neopharmaphobia — fear of new drugs
• Osmophobia — fear of smells
• Panphobia — fear of everything
• Pentheraphobia — fear of mother-in-law
• Phobophobia — fear of fear itself
• Polyphobia — fear of many things
• Psychophobia — fear of the mind
• Sinistrophobia — fear of things "of the left"/left-handed
• Sitophobia — fear of food or eating
• Sophophobia — fear of learning
• Tridecaphobia — fear of the number 13

From: **The Encyclopedia of Phobias, Fears and Anxieties**
R. Doctor, Ph.D. & A. Khan
Facts on File, Inc.; New York, 1989

Obsessive-Compulsive Disorder

Obsessive-Compulsive Disorder (OCD) is characterized by:
• **obsessions** — recurrent thoughts, impulses or images
• **compulsions** — conscious, repetitive behaviors or mental acts
OCD can be diagnosed by the presence of either obsessions or compulsions. Obsessions are recognized as products of the patient's own mind (as opposed to **thought insertion**). The intrusive nature of obsessions causes anxiety, which is lessened by carrying out the compulsion.

Biological Features
• **Serotonin** dysregulation is the leading hypothesis
• Intractable OCD is treated by lesioning the **cingulum**
• About 35% of patients have affected family members
• About 25% of OCD patients have **tics**, and 25% of patients with tics have OCD (both involve the basal ganglia)

Psychosocial Features
• The lifetime prevalence of OCD is about 2% (equal sex ratio)
• OCD differs from the Obsessive-Compulsive Personality Disorder; most OCD patients do not have this personality disorder premorbidly
• The major ego defenses used in OCD are: **isolation** (of affect), **undoing**, **magical thinking**, and **intellectualization**
• Learning theory proposes that compulsions, like phobias, are conditioned stimuli

Biological Treatment
• Serotonin reuptake inhibitors are used; the treatment of choice is **clomipramine** and the **SSRIs**; the doses required are similar to those used to treat depressive disorders
• **MAOIs**, **buspirone**, **neuroleptics** and **fenfluramine** are also used; augmentation with **lithium** has also been successful

Psychosocial Treatment
• **Exposure** and **Response Prevention** are the behavioral interventions most frequently used
• Psychodynamic approaches focus on the handling of impulses

Prognosis
• The prognosis for OCD is generally favorable; about 70% of patients have at least moderate improvement in their symptoms

Obsessive-Compulsive Disorder

"FORCED A BIT"

Feels anxious — OCD is an Anxiety Disorder

Obsessions

Recognizes obsessions are a product of own mind

Compulsions

Excessive nature of obsessions and compulsions is appreciated

Distressing to the patient (ego-dystonic)

Attempts are made to ignore or suppress obsessions

Behaviors are not realistically connected with the obsession

Interferes with normal routine (social or occupational functioning)

Time consuming — takes up more than 1 hour per day

 OCD Tidbits

• OCD symptoms generally follow certain themes (listed in decreasing order of frequency):

Obsession	Corresponding Compulsion
• contamination	• cleaning (of self or articles)
• doubt (impending doom)	• checking (stoves, locks, etc.)
• intrusive derogatory, aggressive or sexual thoughts	• usually occur without compulsions, may involve mental acts
• symmetry, neatness, precision	• perfection, leading to obsessional slowness

• Compulsions are usually behaviors, but include mental acts such as repeating phrases or names
• Depressive symptoms and major depressive episodes are common in patients with OCD; non-suppression on the Dexamethasone Suppression Test is seen in 30% of patients with OCD
• Other anxiety disorders and substance-related disorders frequently complicate the course of OCD
• The estimated interval between the onset of symptoms and the decision to seek help is between 5 and 10 years; the usual presentation is to a physician (other than a psychiatrist) for somatic complications (e.g. damaged skin from repeated hand washing)

OCD Tidbits

• Like delusions, obsessions tend to fall into a relatively small number of themes:

Theme	Corresponding Obsession
• Cleanliness	• Contamination
• Order	• Symmetry, Precision
• Sex & Aggression	• Assault, Sexual Assault, Homicide, Insults
• Doubt	• Safety, Catastrophe, Unworthiness

• Another scheme for classifying obsessions is as follows:
• *Intellectual obsessions* — involving philosophical or metaphysical questions about life, the universe & everything; destiny; curved space; gravity waves, etc.
• *Inhibiting obsessions* — doubts or prohibitions about actions which may be harmful to others; the patient may become withdrawn or isolated to ensure such actions do not occur
• *Impulsive obsessions* — urges to steal, collect (hoard), or count (called **arithomania**)

• While obsessions are a cardinal symptom of OCD, they are also seen in:
• Depression — obsessive thoughts about death, illness, a bleak future, self-deprecation, negative view of others, etc.
• Psychotic disorders — the prodrome of schizophrenia (schizophreniform disorder) can include obsessions, which cause the patient to perform unusual rituals
• Other anxiety disorders — such as phobias, where the patient is tormented by thoughts of the feared object or situation when not faced with it
• Obsessive-Compulsive Personality Disorder (OCPD) — shares some features with OCD
• Hypochondriasis — preoccupation with serious illness
• Body Dysmorphic Disorder — intrusive thoughts of image distortion
• Impulse control disorders
• Temporal lobe epilepsy
• Tourette's Disorder
• Organic mental disorders — e.g. traumatic head injuries, carbon monoxide poisoning, disorders of the basal ganglia, cardiovascular accidents

• **Preoccupations** differ from obsessions in that they are a willful return to thinking or conversing about a topic (in a focused manner)
• **Rumination** is another term for an intellectual obsession; here, people "chew" (mull over) their "cud" (thoughts) without achieving a resolution; there is often an irritating and unnecessary quality (both in time and intensity) to this type of thought content

OCD Tidbits

• As mentioned on the last page, obsessions tend to fall within a small number of themes, with aggression, cleanliness and order being the most prominent. In Freud's psychosexual stages of development, these are the issues that dominate the **anal phase**. Control and autonomy are the key outcomes from this stage. Freud linked obsessive behaviors to difficulties during the anal stage of development, and defined the **anal triad** as consisting of parsimoniousness, orderliness and obstinacy (mnemonic — P.O.O.).
• Ego defenses are used to defend against the expression of unfulfilled dependency wishes and strong feelings of anger directed at significant others (usually the parents). The following ego defenses are thought to be operative in OCD:

• **Ambivalence** develops as a result of the simultaneous existence of longing (love) and aggressive wishes (hate). This conflict of opposing emotions paralyzes the patient with doubt and indecision, and can result in the **doing-undoing** pattern seen with obsessions and compulsions.

• **Undoing** involves an action, either verbalization or behavior, that symbolically makes amends for conflicts, stresses or unacceptable wishes. This is the predominant defense contributing to the compulsive component.

• **Magical thinking** is also a component of OCD in that the obsession is given great power, and is seen to be more connected to events than is realistic. For example, having thoughts of a disaster does not make it occur.

• **Isolation (of affect)** separates or strips an idea from its accompanying feeling or affect. This is the predominant defense contributing to the obsessive component. An idea is made conscious, but the feelings are kept within the unconscious. When this defense is used to a lesser degree, three others mechanisms may be used:
  • Intellectualization — excessive use of abstract thinking
  • Moralization — morality isolates contradictory feelings
  • Rationalization — justification of unacceptable attitudes

• **Reaction Formation** transforms an impulse into a diametrically opposed thought, feeling or behavior. This is frequently seen as a "counter-dependent" attitude in which patients (primarily with obsessive-compulsive personalities) eradicate dependency on anyone or anything. Similarly, maintenance of a calm exterior guards against an awareness of angry feelings. For example, orderliness is a reaction formation against the childhood desire to play with feces or to make a mess.

• **Displacement** redirects feelings from a conflict or stressor onto a symbolically related, but less threatening, person or object. "Kicking the dog" or "shooting the messenger" are examples of this defense.

Posttraumatic Stress Disorder

Posttraumatic Stress Disorder (PTSD) is a reaction to a severe stressor that is out of usual human experience. Frequently, the traumatic event is a war, assault, natural disaster or accident. PTSD involves symptoms in each of 3 sets of reactions:
• persistent reexperience of the event
• persistent avoidance of stimuli associated with the trauma
• symptoms of increased arousal

Biological Features
• Hyperactivity of the hypothalamic-pituitary-adrenal axis
• Persistent elevations of blood pressure and heart rate
• Pathways from the **locus ceruleus** (noradrenergic transmission) mediate the symptoms of hyperarousal
• Temperamental/genetic factors influence the response to stress

Psychosocial Features
• PTSD has a prevalence of 1%; there are no gender differences
• PTSD is endemic in some groups (e.g. combat veterans)
• This disorder is a combination of *attempts to master the trauma through repetition* and *attempts to avoid such repetition*
• The traumatic event may awaken previously unresolved conflicts and reactivate primitive instinctual drives

Biological Treatment
• There is no clear pharmacologic treatment of choice for PTSD
• Treatment of depression or anxiety symptoms is recommended
• Many other medications have been given anecdotal support

Psychosocial Treatment
• Cognitive-behavioral approaches have been established; the initial focus in on **relaxation training**; hypnosis is also used
• Psychodynamic approaches may involve **abreaction** of the initial event (as in the movie ORDINARY PEOPLE)
• Education about PTSD (especially the risk of developing a substance-related disorder) and group therapy are helpful

Prognosis
• The prognosis is variable; over 75% of patients either recover or have mild symptoms; 10% have chronic severe symptoms
• The old and young tend to have a more complicated course
• Preexisting psychiatric conditions worsen the prognosis

Posttraumatic Stress Disorder

"PRIDE AFRAID CHASSIS"

Physiologic reactivity when exposed to cues
Recollections of the event that are distressing
Internal cues cause distress (symbolic reminder) } reexperience of the event
Dreams of the event that are distressing
External cues cause distress

Avoids stimuli associated with the trauma
Foreshortened future — no long-term goals
Recall of the event is impaired } avoidance of stimuli
Affect has a restricted range
Interest in activities is diminished
Detached from others

Concentration is impaired
Hypervigilance
Angry outbursts } increased arousal symptoms
Sleep disturbance — trouble staying asleep
Startle response is exaggerated
Insomnia — trouble falling asleep
Significant impairment in functioning

 PTSD Tidbits

• The presence of emotional vulnerability or preexisting psychopathology predisposes individuals to develop PTSD
• PTSD has historically been called **Soldier's Heart**, **DaCosta's Heart** (from a description of Civil War casualties) & **Shell Shock**
• The severity of the stressor does not necessarily correlate with symptom severity; the person's subjective response is the key
• PTSD must be present for at least one month to be diagnosed
• Symptoms lasting less than 4 weeks but at least 2 days, are diagnosed as an **Acute Stress Disorder**

Generalized Anxiety Disorder

Generalized Anxiety Disorder (GAD) is characterized by excessive and pervasive worry accompanied by physical symptoms. The anxiety is not confined to the symptoms of another clinical disorder (e.g. being anxious about public speaking, as in Social Phobia). Anxiety involves worry without an awareness of cause; anxiety with a known cause is called fear.

Biological Features
• Genetic factors are not yet well understood in GAD
• There is (some) genetic and (good) clinical evidence that MDE and GAD exist on a spectrum of expression; these disorders frequently coexist
• Peripherally, anxiety is manifested by the sympathetic nervous system; in the CNS, the neurotransmitters involved are GABA, serotonin, norepinephrine, glutamate, and possibly others

Psychosocial Features
• GAD has a lifetime prevalence of 5%; women are diagnosed approximately twice as often as men
• **Winnicott** — failure of the parental **holding environment**
• **Freud** — anxiety is a signal to the ego that an instinctual urge is pressing for expression
• **Stack Sullivan** — interpersonal source of anxiety stems from fear related to disapproval

Biological Treatment
• Site of action is a complex consisting of a **benzodiazepine receptor**, **GABA$_A$ receptor** and **chloride channel**; neuronal hyperpolarization reduces the firing rate and decreases anxiety
• **Buspirone** is an effective anxiolytic
• MAOIs, TCAs, antihistamines and beta-blockers are also used

Psychosocial Treatment
• Cognitive-behavioral approaches have been established; the initial focus is on **relaxation training** (also **biofeedback**)
• Psychodynamic approaches search for source of anxiety

Prognosis
The prognosis for GAD depends on the presence of:
• perpetuating factors — removing their influence can improve prognosis
• comorbid conditions (e.g. MDE, Panic Disorder) — worsen the prognosis

Generalized Anxiety Disorder

"I'M A FICKLE CASE"

Impaired functioning

Muscle tension

Axis I condition, if coexisting, is not the focus of the anxiety

Fatigued

Irritable

Control of worry is difficult

Keyed up (edgy)

Lasts for at least six months, occurs more days than not

Events and activities are focus of the worry (not just a single focus)

Concentration is impaired

Anxiety is excessive

Sleep disturbance

Excluded — Substance Disorders & General Medical Conditions

GAD Tidbits

• GAD is often precipitated by a psychosocial stressor
• **Buspirone** appears to be less useful if benzodiazepines have been used recently
• The **Dexamethasone Suppression Test** is often positive in GAD
• Cardiac, endocrine and neurologic illnesses are among the most common medical causes of anxiety disorders
• Tolerance does not appear to develop to the anxiolytic effects of **benzodiazepines**; however, addiction is a long-term concern
• **Angst** is the German word for fear; the initial translations of Freud's work used it as a replacement for anxiety
• Freud used the term **anxiety neurosis** to refer to both GAD and Panic Disorder
• **Separation anxiety, castration anxiety** and **superego anxiety** are important psychological factors in the etiology of anxiety disorders

Somatization Disorder

Somatization Disorder (SD) is characterized by the presence of multi-system physical complaints that cannot be explained medically. If a medical condition exists, then the reported symptoms are excessive for the degree of pathology present. This disorder is also called **Briquet's Syndrome**.

Biological Features
• Male relatives of females with SD have an increased risk of **Antisocial Personality Disorder** and **Substance-Related Disorders**; female relatives have an increased prevalence of SD
• There may be alterations in the processing of information from somatic sources; "somatizing" patients may habitually focus on, and emphasize, minor physical sensations

Psychosocial Features
• Lifetime prevalence for women is 0.5%; SD is at least 5 times more common in women; cultural factors may influence development
• Childhood abuse may predispose to SD later in life
• **Somatization** is an ego defense mechanism in which repressed instinctual urges are converted into physical symptoms
• Somatization behavior may be a strategy to get attention that wouldn't be given for emotional problems

Biological Treatment
• Distinguishing legitimate symptoms from somatized complaints is crucial; SD patients can and do develop serious illnesses
• Once the above distinction has been made, what *is not* done (i.e. investigations) is as important as what *is* done
• Depression and anxiety disorders are the two most common coexisting conditions that require pharmacologic treatment

Psychosocial Treatment
• Coordination by one physician is preferable
• Searching for the emotional component in symptom formation helps patients develop a vocabulary for expressing feelings

Prognosis
• SD is a chronic condition, and one of the few diagnoses with an age stipulation (onset prior to age 30); the course fluctuates, often with a change in symptoms instead of their disappearance

Somatization Disorder

"FOOT PAINS"

Four pain symptoms
One sexual symptom
One pseudoneurological symptom
Two gastrointestinal symptoms

Physical complaints are in excess of actual medical conditions
Age of onset under 30 years
Investigations do not reveal a cause for the complaints
Not due to malingering or factitious disorder
Social, occupational or academic functioning is affected

 SD Tidbits

• SD occurs more frequently in patients:
  • from lower socio-economic groups
  • with less education and intelligence
  • with avoidant, passive-aggressive, self-defeating or obsessive-compulsive personality traits and disorders
• Involvement in a form of psychotherapy has been reported to lessen medical expenses by half
• Societal roles or expectations may account for the gender discrepancy seen in SD; another hypothesis is that a common genotype or histrionic temperament is manifested as SD in women and Antisocial Personality Disorder in men
• Another mnemonic for SD is based on 7 screening questions developed by Othmer & DeSouza*

• **S**hortness of breath (without exertion)	**S**omatization
• **D**ysmenorrhea	**D**isorder
• **B**urning in sexual organs or rectum	**B**esets
• **L**ump in throat	**L**adies
• **A**mnesia	**A**nd
• **V**omiting	**V**exes
• **P**ain in the extremities	**P**hysicians

* Othmer & DeSouza: *A Screening Test for Somatization Disorder*
American Journal of Psychiatry, **142**: p.1146-9, 1985

Conversion Disorder

"MISSES GULPS"

Motor symptoms that are under voluntary control
Investigations do not reveal identifiable pathology
Sensory symptoms that are under voluntary control
Symptoms are not limited only to pain or sexual function
Experience is out of keeping with cultural norms
Social, occupational or other abilities are impaired

Gain needs to be considered (**primary** and **secondary gain**)
Unintentional production — not Factitious Disorder or Malingering
La belle indifférence — patient is unconcerned about deficits
Psychological factors are associated with onset of symptoms
Somatization Disorder excluded

Conversion Disorder Tidbits

• Conversion implies that an unconscious conflict is "converted" into physical symptoms, often with a symbolic connection to the conflict (for example, a wish to punch someone would be manifested as an inability to use the punching arm)
• The prevalence varies widely, but it is likely less than 1%
• Conversion Disorder is more prevalent in patients with personality disorders, lower intelligence and education, and those chronic psychiatric illnesses
• **Primary gain** is the intrapsychic advantage achieved by keeping the conflict from conscious awareness; **secondary gain** is an external or "real world" advantage bestowed on the patient through removal from the precipitating situation
• Patients frequently model their symptoms after an illness suffered by someone close to them (called **identification**)
• An **amytal interview** (intravenous barbiturate) can produce a temporary diminution of conversion symptoms
• Symptoms often abate within a few days without any specific treatment; of note is that many patients go on to develop legitimate neurological conditions in the future

Hypochondriasis

"DRIPS"

Delusional intensity of thoughts is not present

Reassurance does not lessen the patient's concern

Impairment in social or occupational functioning

Preoccupation with idea of having a serious illness

Six-month minimum duration

Hypochondriasis is the persistent fear of being afflicted with a serious illness. The fear is unfounded, and based on a misinterpretation of bodily symptoms. The term means "below the ribs" and was so named due to the frequency of GI complaints.

 Hypochondriasis Tidbits

• Hypochondriacal patients may have a constitutional sensitivity to somatic symptoms (i.e. a low pain threshold)

• While hypochondriasis is listed as an ego defense, it can be broken down into the components of **repression** (which keeps the conflict from awareness) and **displacement** (which shifts the focus of conflict from the target back onto the patient)

• Hypochondriasis can be thought of as an internal "death sentence" for the guilt felt over aggressive impulses towards another person; it may also serve as a mechanism of atonement for an unacceptable impulse or act*

• Hypochondriasis can be considered a disorder of perception*

• Depression and anxiety disorders frequently coexist

• Examples of general medical conditions that can be confused with Hypochondriasis are occult neoplasms, multiple sclerosis, myasthenia gravis and connective tissue disorders with multi-system involvement; in order to decrease the amount of egg worn on one's face, a thorough investigation is required

• Treatment usually involves an agreement to coordinate treatment with one doctor who can limit referrals and tests; patients may be interested in groups that focus on chronic illness

* Thanks to **Dr. John Mount**, London, Ontario for his teaching in this area

Factitious Disorder

The hallmark of the Factitious Disorder (FD) is the conscious production of symptoms in order to "assume the sick role." The goal appears to be hospital admission, and to be the focus of clinical investigation and treatment. It is both a fascinating and disturbing disorder. FD is of particular interest in psychiatry, both because of the interest in human motivation and because the symptoms that make up the diagnostic criteria can be faked (sometimes with incredible accuracy).

FD does not appear to be explainable on the basis of an obvious gain. For example, narcotics are much more easily obtainable than entering hospital as a patient feigning a serious illness.

Patients often have a facility with health-care terminology and procedures, and know which symptoms to emphasize. They are often eager to have invasive procedures performed — possibly in the hope that there is a complication or a coincidental finding. The etiology of this disorder remains obscure, but clearly involves profound disturbances in identity and personality formation.

This disorder has also been called **Münchausen's Syndrome**, which is a misnomer because he was more of a raconteur. Other terms used are *Hospital Addiction* and *Pseudologia Fantastica*. Management involves early detection, limiting investigations and avoiding unnecessary medication.

Malingering

Malingering is the conscious production of symptoms for an obvious gain (called **secondary gain**). It is not considered a mental disorder. Common types of secondary gain involve: diminution of responsibility for legal or financial problems; prescription medication abuse; avoiding military service; being relieved of unpleasant responsibilities; disability income; admission to hospital, etc.

Disorder	Secondary Gain	Conscious Production
Conversion Disorder	—	—
Factitious Disorder	—	+
Malingering	+	+

Dissociative Identity Disorder

Multiple Personality Disorder (MPD) was renamed the Dissociative Identity Disorder (DID) in the DSM-IV. The essential feature is the co-existence of two or more distinct identities or personalities that take control of an individual and cause deficits in the recall of information.

Historically, DID has been classified under **Hysterical Neuroses, Dissociative Type**. Renaming this condition re-emphasizes the psychological process producing the different identities, rather than the observable manifestations. Additionally, it implies that a single person manifests different internal and external experiences of "self."

There can be a fascinating variability observed in the **alters**, which can be sufficiently well defined to be considered separate "personalities." The alters can have distinct: names; sexual identities and orientation; voices; facility with foreign languages; handedness and handwriting. Amazingly, each can have distinct illnesses, EEGs, eyeglass prescriptions and even allergies!

The usual arrangement involves a dominant personality that is aware of all of the fragments, though this is not usually the personality that seeks treatment. Alters appear to be variably aware of one another. The total number of personalities has been reported to exceed 50, with the average being in the range of 10 to 12. Frequently, the personalities have some connection with one another. For example, all of the persons involved in a traumatic episode (victim, perpetrator, witness, etc.) can be embodied by different personalities. Also, dichotomous personalities (e.g. a good-evil pairing) are often present.

The duality of human nature has often been portrayed using multiple personality themes. A classic example is Robert Louis Stevenson's *Dr. Jekyll and Mr. Hyde*, which has been made into several movie versions. Films have also been made from real cases, in particular *The Three Faces of Eve* and *Sybil*.

Anorexia Nervosa

The hallmark of Anorexia Nervosa (AN) is a refusal to maintain a weight of at least 85% of that expected by age and height on normal growth curves. Despite a state of emaciation, patients with AN have an intense fear of gaining weight due to a distorted perception of their body image.

Biological Features
• The physical effects are those seen with starvation
• May be genetically linked to mood disorders and substance abuse

Psychosocial Features
• AN is more common in developed countries and is 15 times more common in females; the prevalence is about 0.5%
• Patients may strive for autonomy and independence from parents who are (or are perceived to be) over-controlling
• AN fosters the regression to a state in which the demands and expectations of adulthood are not present

Biological Treatment
• Hospitalization may be necessary to prevent death from dehydration, electrolyte disturbances or cardiac arrhythmias
• The possible role of endogenous opiates in maintaining a state of starvation has prompted the use of opiate antagonists
• **Antidepressants, neuroleptics** and **cyproheptadine** are used

Psychosocial Treatment
• **Behavioral Management (Modification)** with Family Therapy and Education on an inpatient unit is a common starting point
• Patients are usually secretive about their exercising, vomiting and unusual eating habits; meals in a group setting and restricting access to washrooms afterwards inhibits many behaviors
• Outpatient cognitive, psychodynamic or family therapy is used

Prognosis
• The prognosis for AN is generally unfavorable; preoccupation with food persists even at a normal body weight
• Mortality rates are in excess of 10% for patients who do not achieve a normal body weight
• Overall psychosocial adjustment remains compromised; long-term relationships and social supports are difficult to maintain

Anorexia Nervosa

"I FEAR LARD"

Image of body is distorted — an abnormality of perception

Fear of gaining weight is intense

Expected weight gains are not made

Amenorrhea — 3 consecutive menstrual cycles missed

Refusal to gain weight

Laxative use — Binge Eating/Purging Type

Anhedonia — high prevalence of mood symptoms

Restricting Type

Denial — of weight loss or emaciated body shape

 Anorexia Nervosa Tidbits

• "Anorexia" is a misnomer for this condition; appetite is usually not lost — patients willfully restrict their food intake
• Patients often have an intense interest in food, and cook elaborate meals for others, collect recipes, etc.
• AN has many components of an obsessive-compulsive disorder regarding food (obsession) and weight loss (compulsion)
• Patients are adept at hiding food; it is frequently cut into small pieces or concealed to give the illusion of consumption
• Quantities of food are often sequestered in hiding places, carried in clothing or purses, or are stolen from stores on impulse
• Aside from the perceptual aberration regarding body shape, the MSE is usually unremarkable
• More than half of patients retain abnormal eating patterns or develop chronic anorexia; poor prognostic factors include:
  • Comorbid Bulimia Nervosa
  • Binge Eating/Purging Type
  • Mood disorder or OCD co-existing with AN
  • Older age of onset
  • Poor premorbid adjustment
  • Coexisting general medical conditions
  • Severe somatic complications
  • Lack of social supports

Bulimia Nervosa

The hallmark of Bulimia Nervosa (BN) is recurrent ingestion of large quantities of food (binge eating), over which patients feel they lack a sense of control. Subsequently, there is a dysphoric state (guilt, disgust, depression — the so-called "post-binge anguish"), which is followed by some type of compensation for the high caloric intake.

Biological Features
• Several medical complications can occur
• Endorphin levels may increase following purging
• BN may have a connection to mood disorders, impulse-control disorders and Borderline Personality Disorder

Psychosocial Features
• BN is more common than AN; the female/male ratio is 10:1
• Psychodynamic factors are thought to be similar to AN; parents may be (or be seen as) more neglectful than controlling
• Bulimic patients lack superego control and externalize their conflicts with impulsive and self-damaging behavior (promiscuity, shoplifting, substance abuse, suicide attempts, etc.)

Biological Treatment
• Hospitalization is not needed as frequently as with AN
• Use of **antidepressants** is indicated; several have shown efficacy (particularly fluoxetine, and also MAOIs, TCAs) independent of the presence of a mood disorder
• **Mood stabilizers** have also been used with success

Psychosocial Treatment
• Psychotherapy (cognitive-behavioral, psychodynamic or family) on an outpatient basis suffices for most patients
• Comorbidity with other conditions makes this a challenging disorder to treat; BN often requires prolonged therapy

Prognosis
• The prognosis for BN is generally better than for AN; a typical course is that of waxing and waning; at the five-year point, one third are doing well, one third have some symptoms, one third do poorly
• Occasional binge eating has been reported in almost half of college-age women; this appears to spontaneously remit in most cases without further episodes or complications

Bulimia Nervosa

"A BINGE"

Average 2 binges/week over 3 months

Behavior after consumption compensates for ingestion*
Ingestion of large amounts of food (binge eating)
Not occurring exclusively during Anorexia Nervosa
Guilty feelings after binge eating
Evaluation of self is unduly based on appearance

 Bulimia Nervosa Tidbits

* Laxatives, cathartics, diuretics, self-induced vomiting, exercise and surreptitious use of thyroid medication are methods used to compensate for the huge caloric load of binge eating

• Bulimia Nervosa is divided into *purging* and *nonpurging types*

• A history of **pica** (eating of non-nutritive substances such as hair or mud) may be present in bulimic patients

• AN and BN patients tend to be high achievers who are concerned with trying to be "perfect" — including body image

• Bulimic patients tend to have better social and sexual adjustment than patients with AN

• The body weight of most BN patients is in the normal range

• Often the texture and consistency of foods make them appealing; popular favorites are smooth, creamy and sweet foods such as pudding, whipped cream or the filling in an Oreo® cookie

• Important general medical conditions are:

  • Kleine-Levin Syndrome (hyperphagia and hypersomnia over a period of weeks, often seen in adolescents, course is self-limiting)

  • Klüver-Bucy Syndrome, which results from limbic system dysfunction, and consists of: visual and auditory agnosia, placidity, hyperorality (exploring items by mouth), hypersexuality and hyperphagia; this can be seen in: Pick's disease, HIV encephalopathy, herpes encephalitis, brain tumors, etc.

Adjustment Disorder

An Adjustment Disorder (AD) is a time limited maladaptive response to an upsetting event (called a **psychosocial stressor**) that is out of proportion to what would be reasonably expected. AD causes significant impairment in an individual's ability to function socially or at work. There are time constraints involved in this diagnosis:

• Symptoms occur within 3 months of the onset of the stressor
• Remission occurs within 6 months of the termination of the stressor, or the consequences of the stressor

AD is not diagnosed if the symptoms can be better explained as an exacerbation of a pre-existing illness. Additionally, symptoms are not severe enough to qualify for the diagnosis of PTSD.

Biological Features
• **Vegetative signs** can be seen when depressed mood is the predominant symptom; physical signs of anxiety can also be seen
• AD can lead to other physical difficulties, such as exacerbation of pre-existing medical illnesses (e.g. cardiac and gastrointestinal)
• Substance-related disorders can develop as a reaction to AD

Psychosocial Features
• AD is common, and is present in up to 20% of inpatients
• The nature of the stressor and its significance to the patient (actual and symbolic) are key considerations
• A patient's previous reaction to stressful situations provides a guide to what may be required to manage the current situation
• Immature coping mechanisms and ego defenses may become obvious during the course of AD

Biological Treatment
• **Antidepressants** and **anxiolytics** may be required for a period

Psychosocial Treatment
• Psychotherapy is the treatment of choice; it can reduce the reaction to the current stressor and decrease recurrences

Prognosis
• The overall outcome is quite favorable; the vast majority of patients resume their previous level of functioning; mood, anxiety or substance-related disorders worsen the prognosis

Adjustment Disorder

"IT'S BAD"

Impairment of social, occupational, academic functioning

Three-month (or less) onset of symptoms from time of stressor

Six-month (or less) duration of symptoms from end of stressor

Bereavement has been excluded

Another **A**xis I diagnosis is excluded

Distress is beyond expectation for the stressor involved

Adjustment Disorder Tidbits

• AD is a diagnosis of exclusion after other Axis I & II disorders have been considered first

• Subtypes of AD are:
- • with depressed mood
- • with anxiety
- • with mixed anxiety and depressed mood
- • with disturbance of conduct
- • with mixed disturbance of emotions and conduct
- • unspecified

• **Uncomplicated Bereavement** involves an *expectable* reaction to a loss; AD involves a reaction *in excess of expectation*

• **PTSD** involves stressors beyond the range of usual human experiences

• Patients with **personality disorders** or **cognitive disorders** are prone to develop AD

• **Brief therapy** and **crisis intervention** are useful psycho-therapies for treating AD

• The DSM-IV contains research diagnoses for conditions called *Minor Depressive Disorder* and *Recurrent Brief Depressive Disorder* in Appendix B; should these conditions be adopted as formal diagnoses, many patients currently diagnosed with Adjustment Disorder with Depressed Mood will receive these diagnoses instead

• AD used to be called a *Transient Situational Disturbance* or a *Transient Situational Personality Disorder*

Impulse-Control Disorders

Impulse-Control Disorders are listed separately in the DSM-IV. They consist of behaviors with the following common elements:
• an urge, impulse or temptation is too strong to resist
• the resulting action harms the person, someone else or property
• an increasing degree of tension is experienced before the act
• there is a release of tension and gratification during the act
• the act is not committed for an obvious goal, such as needing to eat, revenge, dire financial circumstances, etc.

The impulses can be conscious or unconscious. Some patients experience remorse for their actions, but at the time, the impulse is carried out in an **ego-syntonic** manner (i.e. it doesn't distress the patient, see also p. 96). Psychosocial theories postulate a fixation at Freud's oral stage of development. These individuals are needy or "hungry" and may engage in these behaviors to get attention and perhaps love from others. Another possibility is that these actions mediate strong feelings of depression, anxiety or guilt.

Biological theories focus on the similarities between impulsivity and temporal lobe epilepsy. Additionally, patients with head trauma, mental retardation and attention-deficit/hyperactivity disorder appear to manifest these behaviors more frequently. Decreased levels of serotonin and its metabolites have been correlated with violent acts.

MNEMONIC —
"KICK
  IN THE
  PANTS
  PSYCHOTHERAPY"

Kleptomania

Intermittent Explosive Disorder

Trichotillomania

Pyromania

Pathological Gambling

Kleptomania Tidbits

• Kleptomanic patients are compelled to commit the act of theft; they do not have a use or need for the stolen object and often have enough money to have purchased the item
• Kleptomania is unplanned, and almost always a solitary act
• Theft of items can be a feature of Schizophrenia, Bulimia Nervosa, Mania, Antisocial and Borderline Personality Disorders
• If you diagnose someone with kleptomania, don't tell him/her to "take something" for it

 Intermittent Explosive Tidbits

• Intermittent Explosive Disorder (IED) often involves a stressor that causes the patient to feel helpless, useless or frustrated
• The resulting physical outburst is far out of proportion to the stressor, and the recall of the episode is frequently poor
• The patient's personality is not otherwise aggressive
• The personal history often reveals early deprivation, a violent caregiver and substance abuse by a parent or caregiver
• Predisposing factors also include head trauma, cerebral infections, ADHD; soft neurologic signs and EEG changes are also present
• Treatment includes lithium, carbamazepine, dilantin and SSRIs

 Trichotillomania Tidbits

• Human hair is a remarkably resilient substance, and if swallowed can form a **bezoar** which can lead to intestinal obstruction
• Trichotillomania has many features in common with OCD
• Many medications and therapies have been tried for this disorder

 Pyromania Tidbits

• Cruelty to animals, truancy, delinquency and enuresis are common historical features; these patients are almost exclusively male
• There is often a fascination with fire, fire-fighting equipment and flammable compounds
• No obvious gain exists for the person to set the fire

 Pathological Gambling Tidbits

• A support group called Gamblers Anonymous (GA) is available
• Many of the predisposing factors for depression are also seen here (e.g. loss of a parent, divorce, poverty, harsh discipline, etc.)

Personality Disorder Overview

One definition of personality is *a relatively stable and enduring set of characteristic behavioral and emotional traits.* Over time, a person will interact with others in a reasonably predictable way. However, as the adage "don't judge a book by its cover" warns, circumstances can alter behavior so that someone does something "out of character." For example, extreme circumstances like divorce or New Year's Eve can bring out behavior that is atypical for that person.

A **personality disorder** is a variant, or an extreme set of characteristics, that goes beyond the range

Personality or Personality Disorder?

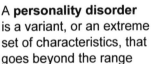

found in most people. The DSM-IV (p. 629) defines a personality disorder as, "*An enduring pattern of inner experience and behavior that deviates markedly from the expectations of the individual's culture, is pervasive and inflexible, has an onset in adolescence or early adulthood, is stable over time, and leads to distress or impairment.*"

While many other definitions exist, points consistently emphasized in defining a personality disorder are that it:
• is deeply ingrained and has an inflexible nature
• is maladaptive, especially in interpersonal contexts
• is relatively stable over time
• significantly impairs the ability of the person to function

Personality disorders are **ego-syntonic**, meaning that behaviors do not distress the person directly, but make more of an impact on those close to the person.

Personality Disorder Overview

Personality Disorders (PDs), like all psychiatric conditions, involve aberrations of perception, thinking, feeling and behavior. These diagnoses are recorded on **Axis II** of the DSM-IV multiaxial system, which is also used to record:
• Mental Retardation
• Prominent personality traits and defense mechanisms, e.g. if a patient meets most of the criteria for a Paranoid Personality Disorder, this is recorded as *Paranoid Personality Features.*
• If a patient uses **defense mechanisms** to a maladaptive level, this is recorded as *Frequent Use of (Defense Mechanism)*
• Other coding for Axis II can be *No Diagnosis* or *Diagnosis Deferred*

The DSM-IV divides Personality Disorders into three clusters based on descriptive or phenomenologic similarities:

Cluster A — Odd or Eccentric ("Mad")
Paranoid, Schizoid, Schizotypal

Cluster B — Dramatic, Emotional or Erratic ("Bad")
Antisocial, Borderline, Histrionic, Narcissistic

Cluster C — Anxious or Fearful ("Sad")
Avoidant, Dependent, Obsessive-Compulsive

The diagnosis of **Personality Change Due to a Medical Condition** is made when a personality disturbance is due to the direct physiologic effects of a medical condition. This personality change must be a clear and persistent change from previous patterns.
• Some of the common manifestations are: aggression, lability, apathy, suspiciousness, poor judgment, or impulsivity
• When this is given as the diagnosis, it is coded on Axis I as: *"Personality Change Due to (Condition),* with the medical condition specified on Axis III

The Paranoid, Schizoid, Schizotypal and Antisocial Personality Disorders are not diagnosed if they are coincident with certain Axis I conditions. Exclusion criteria are not listed for the other personality disorders. The Antisocial Personality Disorder is the only diagnosis with an age requirement and a prerequisite diagnosis. Patients must be at least age eighteen, and have met the criteria for a diagnosis of **Conduct Disorder** before age fifteen.

Psychodynamic Principles

There are some key principles that form the basis of psycho-dynamic psychiatry and give a theoretical approach to the diagnosis and treatment of PDs. The presence of the **unconscious** is an integral part. Dreams and Freudian Slips (**parapraxes**) are the two most common ways the unconscious is accessed.

Experiences in childhood are considered crucial in the formation of the adult personality. It is in these early years that the interactions with caregivers can predispose people to develop personality disorders. Early patterns of relating to others persist into adult life; in a sense, the past repeats itself. This was aptly put by William Wordsworth as, "The child is the father of the man."

Transference

In therapy, the process of transference involves patients experiencing the therapist as though he or she is a significant person from their. Feelings, thoughts and wishes that are "projected" onto the therapist arise from previous significant relationships. In this way, the current therapeutic relationship is a repetition of the past.

Two key points bear emphasis:
• The relationship is *re-enacted* in therapy, not just *remembered*; this becomes more obvious when one pays attention to the process of the session in addition to the content
• The reaction to the therapist is inappropriate and anachronistic

Countertransference

Transference

Psychodynamic Principles

Countertransference

Harry Stack Sullivan said "we are all much more human than otherwise." Just as patients exhibit transference in their relationships with therapists, the converse also happens. Therapists are (usually) human beings who, to some degree, unconsciously experience the patient as someone from their past. Kernberg (1965) described it as "the therapist's conscious and appropriate total emotional reaction to the patient."

Whereas patients' transference is grounds for observation and interpretation, countertransference is not openly discussed in therapy. Constant internal scrutiny is required on the part of the therapist to be aware of countertransference. Though it can be tempting to act on it, doing so only causes a repetition of other relationships. Instead, countertransference can be used diagnostically and therapeutically. It gives a firsthand awareness of how patients interact with others.

Resistance

In therapy, there is a strong drive to oppose the treater's efforts and preserve the psychic status quo. Resistance is as common as transference and should be expected in therapy. Whereas ego defenses are unconscious and are inferred, resistance can be conscious or unconscious and is openly observed. It can take many forms: lateness or absence from sessions, prolonged silence, digression to irrelevant material, questions of a personal nature about the therapist, "forgetting" the content of past sessions, failure to arrange payment, non-compliance, etc.

Resistance is a self-protective mechanism against experiencing strong emotions. Just as countertransference is used therapeutically and not acted upon, resistance also provides important information about the patient. A psychodynamic understanding provides an opportunity to discover *what* the resistance conceals and *what* past situation is being reenacted in therapy. Resistance in a sense is a misnomer. Though the term implies that it impedes treatment, understanding resistance is a large part of the treatment. While medications are used to some extent, by far the majority of interventions are made with various forms of psychotherapy.

Ego Defenses

Freud developed his **topographical theory** which divided the mind into the Conscious, Unconscious and Preconscious. The unconscious mind contains wishes seeking fulfillment that are closely related to instinctual drives, specifically sexual and aggressive urges. A type of thinking called **primary process** is associated with the unconscious. Primary process is not bound by logic, permits contradictions to coexist, contains no negatives, has no regard for time, and is highly symbolized. This is seen in dreams, psychosis and children's thinking.

The preconscious and conscious mind use **secondary process** thinking. This is logical and deals with the demands of external reality. Secondary process is the goal-directed day-to-day type of thinking that adults use.

Over time, Freud incorporated his findings into a new **structural theory**, which was a model containing the **Id**, **Ego** and **Superego**. Present from birth, the **id** is completely unconscious and seeks gratification of instinctual (mainly sexual and aggressive) drives. The **superego** forms from an identification with the same-sex parent at the resolution of the **oedipal conflict**. It suppresses instinctual aims, serves as the moral conscience in dictating what *should not* be done, and, as the ego ideal, dictates what *should* be done.

The **ego** is the mediator between two groups: the id and superego; and the person and reality. A fundamental concept in ego psychology is one of *conflict* among these three agencies. The id, ego and superego battle for expression and discharge of sexual and aggressive drives. This conflict produces anxiety, specifically called **signal anxiety**. This anxiety alerts the ego that a **defense mechanism** is required, which is an unconscious role of the ego.

Ego Defenses

"BUD HAS PRICE"

Blocking

Undoing

Displacement, Denial, Distortion, Dissociation

Hypochondriasis, Humor

Acting Out, Altruism, Anticipation, Asceticism

Sublimation, Suppression, Schizoid Fantasy, Somatization

Projection, Projective Identification, Passive-Aggressive Behavior, Primitive Idealization

Rationalization, Reaction Formation, Repression, Regression

Identification, Idealization, Introjection, Inhibition, Intellectualization, Isolation of Affect

Controlling

Externalization

 Ego Defense Tidbits

• Ego defense mechanisms are **unconscious** processes recruited in response to an internal or external threat; **repression** is the primary defense and others are used when it becomes overwhelmed

• Personality Disorders can be characterized by *which* ego defenses are used, and the *extent* to which they are used

• The following are considered conscious roles of the ego
  • Perception (sense of reality)
  • Reality testing (adaptation to reality)
  • Motor control
  • Intuition
  • Memory
  • Affect
  • Thinking (the ego uses secondary process) and Learning
  • Control of instinctual drives (delay of immediate gratification)
  • Synthetic functions (assimilation, creation, coordination)
  • Language and Comprehension

Antisocial Personality Disorder

"CALLOUS MAN"

Conduct disorder before age 15;
   Current age at least 18

Antisocial acts; commits acts that
   are grounds for **A**rrest

Lies frequently

Lacunae — lacks a superego

Obligations not honored

Unstable — can't plan ahead

Safety of self and others ignored

Money — spouse and children is are not supported

Aggressive, **A**ssaultive

Not occurring exclusively during schizophrenia or mania

Essence of the Antisocial Personality
"A pervasive pattern of disregard for, and violation of, the rights of others." (DSM-IV, 1994)

Ego Defenses
• Controlling   • Projective Identification   • Acting Out   • Dissociation

Antisocial Personality Tidbits

• The Antisocial Personality Disorder (ASPD) is also called the **sociopathic** or **psychopathic personality**

• A seminal book on this personality disorder is called **The Mask of Sanity*** by Dr. Hervey Cleckley (who also co-authored **The Three Faces of Eve**).

   * **The Mask of Sanity, Fifth Edition** is available from:
   Emily S. Cleckley, Publisher
   3024 Fox Spring Road
   Augusta, Georgia
   U.S.A. 30909

Differential Diagnosis

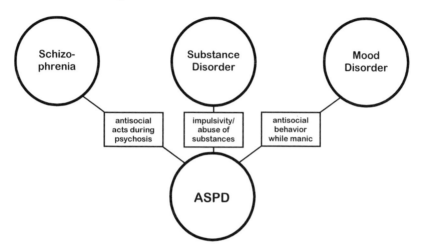

Antisocial Personality Themes

In addition to the diagnostic criteria, the following features become evident in the interview and history:

- Glibness, shallow emotion
- Requires constant stimulation
- Criminal "versatility"
- Parole/probation violations
- Promiscuity
- Juvenile delinquency
- Grandiosity
- Poor impulse control
- Avoids responsibility for actions
- Abuse of substances
- Superior physical prowess
- Behavioral problems as a child
- Social "parasites;" may have several sources of income: "under the table" cash, or profit from stolen property or drugs, disability benefits, etc.

Antisocial Personality Tidbits

- Soft (non-localizing) neurological signs are often present:
    - persistence of primitive reflexes: palmar-mental, grasp, snout, etc.
    - impaired coordination, gait, balance and motor performance
    - graphesthesia, dysdiadochokinesis impaired; positive Romberg sign
- ASPD appears to be genetically related to alcoholism and is frequently complicated by alcohol abuse
- Several factors in childhood are thought to be etiologically significant in the development of ASPD:
    - frequent moves, losses, family break-ups; large families
    - poverty, urban setting, poorly regulated schooling
    - indulgence of material needs, deprivation of emotional needs
    - enuresis, firesetting and cruelty to animals

Avoidant Personality Disorder

"AURICLE"

Avoids activities
Unwilling to get involved
Restrained within relationships
Inhibited in interpersonal situations
Criticism is expected socially
Less than others (self-view)
Embarrassment is the feared
emotion

Essence of the Avoidant Personality
"A pervasive pattern of social inhibition, feelings of inadequacy and hypersensitivity to negative evaluation." (DSM-IV, 1994)

Ego Defenses
• Repression   • Inhibition   • Isolation   • Displacement   • Projection

Avoidant Personality Tidbits

• A forerunner of this diagnosis was called the **inadequate personality disorder**
• Avoidant personalities desire close relationships, but are unduly sensitive to rejection; this is a key point in differentiating avoidant from schizoid personalities, as the latter are presumed not to want intimate relationships
• The Avoidant Personality Disorder (APD) shares considerable overlap with **Social Phobia, Generalized Type**
• APD is often diagnosed in conjunction with other Axis I Disorders (usually anxiety and mood disorders) and other Axis II Disorders (usually schizoid and dependent personality disorders)
• Clark Kent, the mild-mannered reporter who turns into *Superman* (in a telephone booth), is an example of an Avoidant Personality
• MAOIs have been used in anxiety disorders, with phenelzine being the best studied of this group; tricyclic antidepressants, buspirone and β-blockers may be useful
• A "need-fear dilemma" has been hypothesized in this disorder

Differential Diagnosis

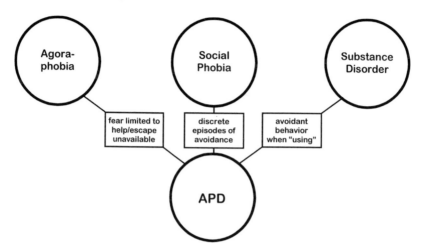

Avoidant Personality Themes
- Feelings of being defective
- Low tolerance for dysphoria
- Self-criticism
- Exaggeration of risks
- Seeks an automatic guarantee of acceptance
- Abrupt topic changes away from personal matters
- Shyness (shame-based avoidance)
- Fear of rejection
- Hypersensitivity to criticism
- "Love at a distance"

Avoidant Personality Tidbits

• APD is one of the character structures most amenable to therapeutic intervention. If patients can endure the initial difficulties in therapeutic situations, they can integrate their growing tolerance for dysphoria into a more assertive approach to other relationships.
• Anxious and inhibited patients share some of the biological features of **Generalized Anxiety Disorder**, particularly hyperarousal of the sympathetic nervous system. Tachycardia, pupillary dilation and laryngeal tightness are common physical signs. Baseline levels of cortisol may also be abnormally high.
• Avoidant patients can be ideal group members and benefit considerably from this type of therapy
• A lifetime of avoiding relationships and social situations can leave patients lacking certain skills. Formal instruction may need to be arranged in areas such as assertiveness training, personal management, sexuality and grooming.

Borderline Personality Disorder

"I RAISED A PAIN"

Identity disturbance

Relationships are unstable

Abandonment frantically
avoided (real or imagined)

Impulsivity

Suicidal gestures (attempts,
threats, self-mutilation)

Emptiness

Dissociative symptoms

Affective instability

Paranoid ideation (stress-related and transient)

Anger is poorly controlled

Idealization followed by devaluation

Negativistic (undermine themselves with self-defeating behavior)

Essence of the Borderline Personality
"A pervasive pattern of instability of interpersonal relationships, self-image, affects and marked impulsivity." (DSM-IV, 1994)

Ego Defenses
• Splitting	• Dissociation	• Denial	• Distortion
• Projective Identification		• Projection	• Acting Out

Borderline Personality Tidbits
• "Borderline" refers to the border between psychosis and neurosis; this disorder was initially called **pseudoneurotic schizophrenia**
• Borderline patients have impaired ego function, and are prone to decompensate under stressful conditions; they also have a poorly developed sense of their own identity (called **identity diffusion**)

Differential Diagnosis

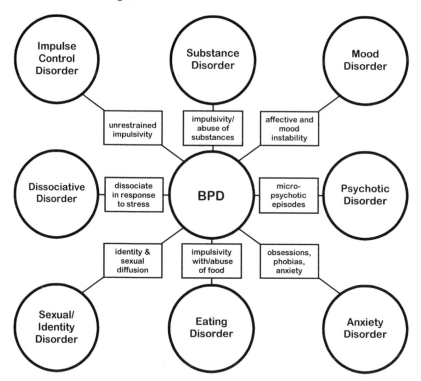

Borderline Personality Themes

- Chaotic childhood
- Parental neglect and abuse
- Self-damaging behavior
- Disrupted education
- Legal difficulties
- Substance abuse or dependence
- Sexual abuse; early onset of sexual activity; promiscuity
- Fears abandonment, maintains self-destructive relationships
- Failure to achieve potential or long-term goals
- Frequent suicidal ideation or gestures (burns, lacerations, etc.)
- Feels hurt by "all" past involvements

▐ Borderline Personality Tidbits

- **Micropsychotic episodes** are brief psychotic breaks that are usually self-limiting and last less than 24 hours
- Glenn Close played a classic borderline personality in *Fatal Attraction*; other good movie examples are *Single White Female, Malicious, The Crush* and *The Hand That Rocks the Cradle*

Dependent Personality Disorder

"NEEDS PUSH"

Needy — other people to assume responsibility for major areas

Expression of disagreement is limited

Excessive need for nurturing

Decision making is difficult

Self-motivation is lacking

Preoccupied with fears of having to care for self

Urgently seeks another relationship when a close one ends

Self-confidence lacking

Helpless when alone

Essence of the Dependent Personality
"A pervasive and excessive need to be taken care of that leads to submissive and clinging behavior and fears of separation." (DSM-IV, 1994)

Ego Defenses
- Idealization
- Inhibition
- Reaction Formation
- Somatization
- Regression
- Projective Identification

 Dependent Personality Tidbits

• A forerunner of this diagnosis was called the **passive-dependent personality**; it was seen as an immature reaction to military stress
• This disorder has also been referred to as the **inadequate personality disorder**
• This disorder has both dependent dimensions (reliance of others, lack of autonomy, diminished self-confidence) and attachment dimensions (maintains closeness to others seen as more powerful)
• Dependent behavior itself is a feature of many other disorders (e.g. borderline and histrionic personalities, mood and anxiety disorders
• DPD has also been described as a **compliant type** of character

Differential Diagnosis

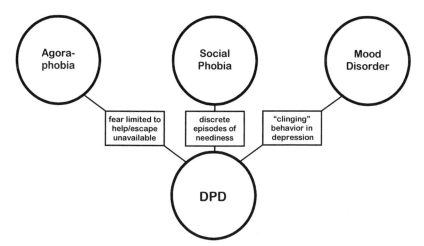

Agora-phobia — fear limited to help/escape unavailable

Social Phobia — discrete episodes of neediness

Mood Disorder — "clinging" behavior in depression

DPD

Dependent Personality Themes
• Neediness
• Rarely lives alone
• Subordinates self
• Works below level of ability
• Continually seeks advice
• Volunteers for unpleasant tasks
• At risk for substance abuse, overmedication, abusive relationships
• Continual involvement in relationships; may endure a difficult one or quickly find another upon dissolution
• May have a "somatic orientation" by expressing their difficulties in terms of physical complaints

Dependent Personality Tidbits

• There are studies to support experiences of both over- and under-indulgence in the childhoods of dependent patients
• DPD contains concepts and criteria for both pathologic degrees of **attachment** and **dependency** behaviors:
   • Attachment behavior in DPD achieves and maintains closeness to a person who is seen as more capable; it is usually aimed at a specific person and increases a sense of security
   • Dependency involves reliance on others, diminished self-confidence and a lack of autonomy; it is a diffuse process that involves seeking protection, help and approval
• Advice, favors and gratification of other needs will not be of long-term benefit in dealing with dependent patients
• The neediness in DPD can manifest itself in substance abuse; alcohol and benzodiazepines in particular can provide a soothing, anxiety-dissolving substitute for attachment

Histrionic Personality Disorder

"I CRAVE SIN"

Inappropriate behavior — seductive or provocative

Center of attention

Relationships are seen as closer than they really are

Appearance is most important

Vulnerable to others' suggestions

Emotional expression is exaggerated

Shifting emotions, **S**hallow

Impressionistic manner of speaking (lacks detail)

Novelty is craved

Essence of the Histrionic Personality
"A pervasive pattern of excessive emotionality and attention seeking." (DSM-IV, 1994)

Ego Defenses
• Repression   • Regression   • Dissociation
• Sexualization   • Denial

 Histrionic Personality Tidbits

• Histrionic replaced the term **hysterical** starting with the DSM-III
• The concept of hysteria now encompasses several disorders: Conversion Disorders, Somatoform Disorders, Dissociative Disorders, Phobias and Amnestic Phenomena
• Histrionic patients relate the "weather" (emotions) instead of the "news" (facts); they also "miss the trees for the forest" in that their impressionistic cognitive style causes them to overlook details
• Psychoanalysis was developed by Freud to treat hysteria; insight-oriented psychotherapies remain the treatment of choice

Differential Diagnosis

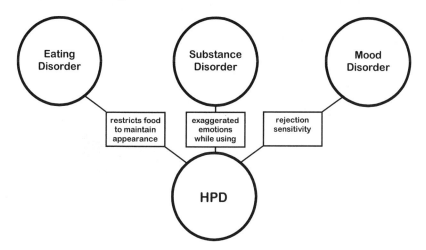

Histrionic Personality Themes
- Emotional instability
- Egocentricity/Vanity
- Suggestibility/Dependence
- Self-dramatization

- Exhibitionism
- Sexual provocativeness
- Fear of sexuality
- Overreaction/Immaturity

Histrionic Personality Tidbits

• Vivien Leigh portrayed excellent examples of this personality as Scarlett O'Hara in *Gone with the Wind*, and as Blanche DuBois in *A Streetcar Named Desire*

• The term histrionic is derived from the Greek word *hustera*, meaning uterus; descriptions of hysterical conditions date back to antiquity when it was thought that the uterus could wander throughout the body causing symptoms at different sites; due to the ambiguity and possible pejorative connotation of the term hysteria, it no longer appears in diagnostic nomenclature

• In the left-brain right-brain scheme, histrionic people are considered to be right-brain dominant; instead of answering questions with details, they give vivid, diffuse, global impressions

• Certain temperamental factors may predispose individuals to a histrionic personality style, such as: intensity, hypersensitivity, extroversion and reward dependence

• Histrionic patients are considered to be fixated in a range between Freud's **oral** and **oedipal stages of development**

Narcissistic Personality Disorder

"A FAME GAME"

Admiration required in excessive amounts

Fantasizes about unlimited success, brilliance, beauty, etc.

Arrogant

Manipulative

Envious of others

Grandiose sense of self-importance

Associates with special people

Me first attitude

Empathy lacking for others

Essence of the Narcissistic Personality
"A pervasive pattern of grandiosity (in fantasy or behavior), need for admiration, and lack of empathy." (DSM-IV, 1994)

Ego Defenses
• Idealization and Devaluation   • Projection   • Identification

 Narcissistic Personality Tidbits

• This personality disorder is less thoroughly validated than other personality disorders; the ICD-10 (International Classification of Diseases published by the WHO) lacks a corresponding diagnosis
• Narcissus was a mythological figure who fell in love with his reflection in a pool of water; Freud brought this term into use
• Narcissistic patients commonly speak "at" instead of "to" others
• Narcissism is a normal developmental state (**primary narcissism**); in adults it is referred to as **secondary narcissism**, and can be a component of other conditions, especially ASPD
• Difficulties arise when patients' grandiosity is confronted with reality; patients can become hostile under such conditions and suffer a **narcissistic injury**, leading to a **narcissistic rage**

Differential Diagnosis

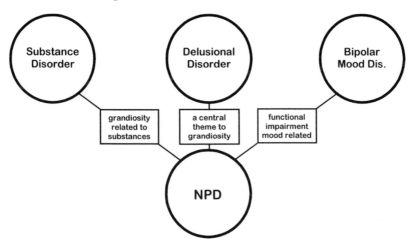

Narcissistic Personality Themes
- Condescending attitude
- Readily blames others
- Dwells on observable assets
- Conspicuous lack of empathy
- Hypersensitive to criticism
- Highly self-referential
- Difficulty maintaining a sense of self-esteem
- Many fantasies, few accomplishments

Narcissistic Personality Tidbits

• **Kernberg** views narcissism as a pathological process involving a "psychic hunger" caused by indifferent parenting; some positive aspect of the child allows an escape from parental threats or spite; this "specialness" facilitates a sense of grandiosity that splits off from the real self, which contains envy, fear and deprivation

• Kohut conceptualized narcissism not as a pathological deviation, but as an arrest in development; the seeds of NPD are sown when caretakers do not validate a child's responses; this empathic failure causes the child to develop an idealized image of the parents, rather than one based on real limits

• Narcissism is a component of several other personality disorders

• NPD can be difficult to validate due to subjectivity of the criteria

• **Reich** recognized that patients protected themselves with **character armor**; he used the term **phallic-narcissist** to refer to individuals who were self-assured, arrogant and protected themselves by attacking others first

Obsessive Compulsive Personality

"PERFECTION"

Preoccupied with details, rules, plans, organization

Emotionally restricted

Reluctant to delegate tasks

Frugal

Excessively devoted to work

Controlling over others

Task completion interfered with by perfectionism

Inflexible

Overconscientious about morals, ethics, values, etc.

Not able to discard belongings; hoards objects

Essence of the Obsessive Compulsive Personality
"A pervasive pattern of preoccupation with orderliness, perfectionism, and mental and interpersonal control, at the expense of openness, flexibility and efficiency." (DSM-IV, 1994)

Ego Defenses
• Undoing   • Reaction Formation   • Displacement
• Isolation of Affect, via
> • Intellectualization
> • Moralization
> • Rationalization

Obsessive-Compulsive Personality Tidbits

• This personality disorder is not a premorbid condition for Obsessive Compulsive Disorder; early descriptions did not differentiate between these conditions (hence the similarity in name); they are now regarded as two clearly different disorders
• Freud defined the **anal triad** as: parsimoniousness, orderliness and obstinacy (p.o.o.); **Reich** called OCPDs "living machines"
• Also referred to as **anankastic** (Greek for "forced") personalities

Differential Diagnosis

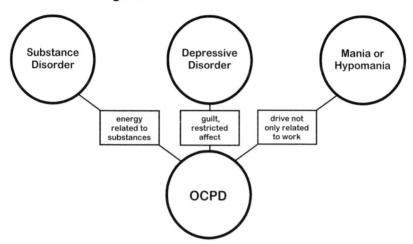

Obsessive-Compulsive Personality Themes
- Emotional constriction
- Indecisiveness
- Fixated on details
- Cerebral rigidity and inflexibility
- Hoards money, objects, etc.
- Few leisure activities; can't relax
- Concerned with results, productivity and achievement
- Humorless; lacks spontaneity
- Answers questions about emotions with thoughts — "It was my *feeling* that my boss was incompetent, I could have done the job in a much more efficient manner."

▉ Obsessive-Compulsive Personality Tidbits

- Obsessive personalities relate the "news" (facts) instead of the "weather" (emotions); they also "miss the forest for the trees" because they are too focused on details to see the big picture
- The classic etiology of OCPD stems from difficulties arising during Freud's **anal stage** of psychosexual development (roughly ages 1-3, corresponding to Erikson's **autonomy vs. shame and doubt**)
- There are no findings describing possible genetic links or physiologic abnormalities in OCPD; no less a proponent than Freud thought that obsessive individuals had a rectal hypersensitivity!
- OCPD appears to be more common in the oldest child in a family
- Cultural influences are etiologically significant; North American society, in particular, rewards independence, hard work, orderliness and punctuality; "Deal with it" and "Just do it" reinforce this

OCD vs. OCPD

Despite the similarity in names, these are phenomenologically distinct conditions. Features that distinguish between the two are:

Feature	OCD	OCPD
Central Concept	Recurrent, intrusive thoughts and/or behaviors/mental acts	Enduring preoccupation with perfection, orderliness and interpersonal control
Subjective Experience	Egodystonic; recognizes irrationality of mental events and behavior	Egosyntonic; doesn't seek help until close relationships are affected or defenses break down
Impact on daily routine	Time consuming; interferes with ability to function	Defends traits and methods as being effective and justified by productivity
Mentation	Aware of forced nature of thoughts, recognize as a product of own mind; resists compulsions	Thoughts lack quality of intrusiveness; behavior occurs automatically, most processes remain unconscious
Manifestations	Often involve themes	Pervasive throughout
Anxiety	Marked; anxious dread	Not usually evident
Etiology	Growing evidence for genetic factors	Psychosocial influences predominate
Biological Features	Abnormal CT & PET scans; some structural abnormalities found	None consistently present
Treatment	Role of serotonin strongly implicated	Psychotherapy in various forms

OCD and OCPD were initially formulated as one disorder, hence the similarity in name. There are conflicting opinions about the degree to which OCPD may be present prior to the onset of OCD. Currently, there is more evidence against this association. OCD is associated with the other Cluster C personality disorders (Dependent and Avoidant) more frequently than it is with OCPD.

Rules of Order for the Malignant Obsessive-Compulsive Personality

• Being a Type A personality isn't good enough, strive for an A⁺.

• When in doubt, think, Think, THINK it out.

• The inkblot test has no time limit. After giving your response, clean up some of the mess.

• The more you do, and the faster you do it, the longer you live.

• If it's worth doing, it's worth overdoing, *right now*!

• The best reward for hard work is more work.

• Encourage others to do it by the book, **your** book.

• Perfection is the lowest acceptable standard.

• You can get all the rest you need when you're dead.

• The words **compromise**, **choice** and **no** are not in your vocabulary.

• If you can't change the rules, change the game.

• Burn the candle at both ends, and in the middle!

Paranoid Personality Disorder

"HEAD FUG"

Hidden meanings read into others' remarks and actions
Exploitation expected from others
Attacks on character are perceived
Doubts loyalty of others

Fidelity of partner questioned
Unjustified doubts about others
Grudges held

Essence of the Paranoid Personality
"A pervasive distrust and suspiciousness of others such that their motives are interpreted as malevolent." (DSM-IV, 1994)

Ego Defenses
• Projection   • Projective Identification   • Denial
• Splitting   • Reaction Formation

 Paranoid Personality Tidbits

• PPD is not diagnosed if it occurs exclusively during the course of schizophrenia, a mood disorder with psychotic features, another psychotic disorder or is due to the direct physiological effects of a general medical condition (DSM-IV,1994)
• Literally translated from Greek, **paranoia** means "a mind beside itself" and has historically been used to refer to a wide number of psychiatric conditions
• Paranoid personalities **do not** have ideas that are of delusional intensity; this is a key feature in distinguishing this personality disorder from Paranoid Schizophrenia and Delusional Disorder
• Paranoid patients are among the most likely to become violent; to maintain rapport and avoid danger, don't challenge their ideas directly; a "let's agree to disagree" approach is one way of handling difficult interview situations
• The term *querulous* means continually complaining or peevish

Differential Diagnosis

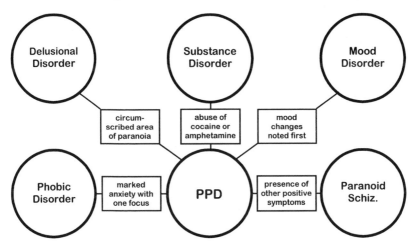

Paranoid Personality Themes

• Externalizes blame for difficulties — sees self as the continual target of abuse; constantly complains about poor treatment
• Repeated difficulty in dealing with authority figures
• Overestimates minor events — "Makes mountains out of molehills"
• Searches intensively to confirm suspicions to the exclusion of more reasonable conclusions — "Misses the forest for the trees"
• Cannot relax; displays little or no sense of humor
• Projects envy or even pathological jealousy — "They're out to get me because they want what I have"
• Critical of those who they see as weaker, needy, or defective
• Difficulty exuding warmth or talking about insecurities

Paranoid Personality Tidbits

• Antipsychotics have been tried but without consistent results
• Brief psychotic episodes (minutes to hours) can occur, but since PPD is not a psychotic disorder, neuroleptics may be needed for short periods only
• PPD can be a premorbid condition to an Axis I disorder
• Paranoid behavior can also be modeled — **folie à deux** is a disorder in which the delusion(s) of one person induce(s) another to believe the idea; though this disorder is usually seen in the context of a delusional or psychotic disorder, it illustrates the power of environmental influences
• Paranoid traits are also associated with developmental handicaps

Schizoid Personality Disorder

"SIR SAFE"

Solitary lifestyle
Indifferent to praise or criticism
Relationships of no interest

Sexual experiences not of interest
Activities not enjoyed
Friends lacking
Emotionally cold and detached

Essence of the Schizoid Personality
"A pervasive pattern of detachment from social relationships and a restricted range of expression of emotions in interpersonal settings." (DSM-IV, 1994)

Ego Defenses
• Schizoid Fantasy   • Intellectualization   • Projection
• Introjection   • Idealization, then Devaluation

Schizoid Personality Tidbits

• This personality disorder is not diagnosed if it occurs exclusively during the course of schizophrenia, a mood disorder with psychotic features, another psychotic disorder, or a pervasive developmental disorder, or is due to the direct physiological effects of a general medical condition (DSM-IV, 1994)
• Schizoid personality disorder overlaps with the **negative symptoms** of schizophrenia (recall that negative symptoms are those *removed* or *missing* from the clinical picture)
• Schizoid personality disorder has a debatable genetic link to schizophrenia; evidence for the link to schizophrenia is stronger for the Schizotypal Personality Disorder
• In psychoanalytic and older psychiatric literature, the term "schizoid" referred to the DSM-IV concepts of schizoid, avoidant and/or schizotypal personalities; these diagnoses were introduced as separate disorders starting with the DSM-III

Differential Diagnosis

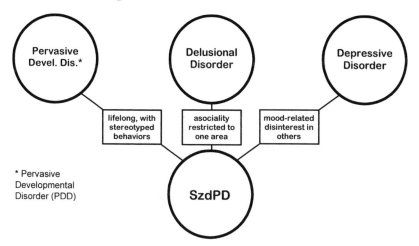

* Pervasive
Developmental
Disorder (PDD)

Schizoid Personality Themes
- Prefers to do things alone
- Why bother? Who cares?
- Withdrawn, reclusive
- Works below potential
- Observer, not participant
- Lacks interests and hobbies
- No apparent desire to pursue relationships
- Deficient motivation
- "Goes through the motions"
- May show considerable creativity
- Aloof, distant, cold
- Humorless
- Constricted emotions

 Schizoid Personality Tidbits

- Families of patients with schizoid personalities have a higher prevalence of schizophrenia, schizotypal and avoidant personality disorder than the general population
- Analytic observations generally hold that men suffer more from disorders characterized by excessive isolation, and women more from disorders of excessive dependence (Dependent Personality Disorder and Depression)
- SzdPD appears to be stable over time
- In his book *Solitude*, Storr emphasizes that many of the world's great thinkers lived alone for the majority of their lives (e.g. Descartes, Newton, Locke, Pascal, Spinoza, Kant, Leibniz, Schopenhauer, Nietzsche, Kierkegaard and Wittgenstein); even among notably creative individuals who did marry, there is an almost universal observation that their work was carried out in solitude

Schizotypal Personality Disorder

"UFO AIDER"

Unusual perceptions
Friendless except for family
Odd beliefs, thinking and speech

Affect is inappropriate or constricted
Ideas of reference
Doubts others — suspicious
Eccentric appearance and behavior
Reluctant in social situations, anxious

Essence of the Schizotypal Personality
"A pervasive pattern of social and interpersonal deficits marked by acute discomfort with, and reduced capacity for, close relationships as well as by cognitive or perceptual distortions and eccentricities of behavior." (DSM-IV, 1994)

Ego Defenses
• Projection   • Distortion   • Primitive Idealization
• Splitting   • Schizoid Fantasy • Denial

Schizotypal Personality Tidbits

• This personality disorder is not diagnosed if it occurs exclusively during the course of schizophrenia, a mood disorder with psychotic features, another psychotic disorder, or a pervasive developmental disorder
• Schizotypal is an abbreviation of **schizophrenic genotype**; this personality disorder is considered a phenotypic variant of the schizophrenic genotype
• Schizotypal personality disorder overlaps with the **positive symptoms** of schizophrenia (positive symptoms are those **added** to the clinical picture — hallucinations, delusions, unusual behavior, a formal thought disorder and inappropriate affect)
• Schizotypal personalities may decompensate under stress and develop **micropsychotic episodes** that last less than 24 hours

Differential Diagnosis

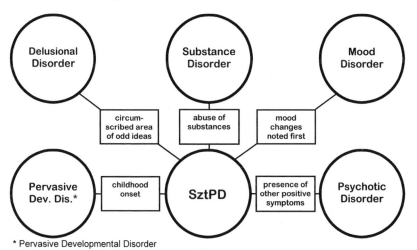

* Pervasive Developmental Disorder

Schizotypal Personality Themes
- Clairvoyance
- Ideas of reference
- Suspiciousness
- Emotional reasoning
- Premonitions
- Alternative/fringe interests
- Existential concerns
- Magical thinking

Schizotypal Personality Tidbits

• As with SzdPD, any disorder that is marked by eccentric behavior, isolation and peculiarities of language needs to be differentiated from: **Autism, Asperger's Disorder, Expressive** and **Mixed Receptive-Expressive Disorders**; language disorders are established by the primacy and severity of language difficulties in relation to other features

• Two conditions (no longer in the DSM) that overlap with SztPD are:
   • **Latent Schizophrenia** — occasional behavioral peculiarities or thought disorders; progression to clear psychotic pathology does not occur; also known as *borderline* or *pseudoneurotic* schizophrenia.
   • **Simple Schizophrenia** — gradual, insidious loss of drive, interest and initiative; vocational performance deteriorates and there is marked social withdrawal; hallucinations or delusions may be present, but only for brief periods of time

• Physiologic findings in schizophrenia may also be abnormal in patients with SztPD (e.g. **saccades, auditory evoked potentials**)

Neuroleptic Indications

"A BATCH O' SPICES"

Acute psychotic disorder

Bipolar Mood Disorder — acute and prophylactic treatment
Aggressive behavior, Agitation
Tourette's Syndrome
Chronic psychotic disorders
Hiccups

Obsessive-Compulsive Disorder

Schizophrenia prophylaxis
Parkinson's Disease (psychotic episodes), Pruritis
Impulsivity
Cocaine withdrawal
Emesis (neuroleptics are potent anti-emetics)
Self-injurious behavior

 Neuroleptic Tidbits

• Flupenthixol in low doses may act as an antidepressant
• Neuroleptics are used in delusional (psychotic) depression
• Typical neuroleptics cause blockade of the dopamine D_2 receptor
• Novel or atypical neuroleptics act on other dopamine receptor subtypes and possibly on other neurotransmitters
• A neuroleptic withdrawal syndrome has been observed; it is more likely to occur with abrupt cessation from high doses
• Dopamine blockade in the **mesolimbic** area is correlated with reducing the positive symptoms of schizophrenia
• Dopamine blockade in the **nigrostriatial** tract causes the movement disorders of extra-pyramidal symptoms (EPS)
• Dopamine blockade in the **tuberoinfundibular** area causes endocrine side effects
• Neuroleptics cause blockade of 5 neurotransmitters ("**HANDS**") — **h**istamine, **a**cetylcholine, **n**orepinephrine, **d**opamine and **s**erotonin

Side Effects of Neuroleptics

"HAPPENS WITH DOPAMINE"

Hepatic — obstructive or cholestatic jaundice

Allergic dermatitis

Prolactin levels increase — amenorrhea/galactorrhea

Photosensitivity — sunburn-like effects

EKG changes — prolonged PR and QT intervals; flattened T waves

Neuroleptic malignant syndrome

Seizure threshold lowered

Weight gain

Impotence and Impairment of other sexual functions

Tardive dyskinesia

Hematologic — leukopenia and agranulocytosis

Dystonic reactions

Orthostatic hypotension

Parkinsonism

Akinesia

Motor restlessness — **akathisia**

Insomnia

Newer antipsychotics cause fewer side effects

Eye changes — short-term and long-term effects[o]

 **Neuroleptic Tidbits**

[o] **Chlorpromazine** can cause pigmentation and granular deposits in the lens and cornea; **thioridazine** can cause irreversible pigmentation of the retina in high doses

• Low serum iron levels may predispose to akathisia, low calcium levels to EPS; temperature regulation can become impaired

• **Pisa Syndrome** and **Rabbit Syndrome** are two late complications of neuroleptic administration

• Teratogenic effects have not been clearly demonstrated

Neuroleptic Malignant Syndrome

"COMMIT HALDOL"

Creatine phosphokinase (CPK) elevation
Onset is related to use of neuroleptics (usually within 7 days)
Mutism
Myoglobinuria — can lead to acute renal failure
Incontinence
Tremor

Hot — temperature can become dangerously elevated
Autonomic dysfunction — BP, pulse and respiratory rate changes
Leukocytosis
Dripping — diaphoresis & salivation
Obtunded — ranges from confused to comatose
Liver function tests may be abnormal

Factors Associated with NMS

"OH DARN"

Organic brain syndromes — mental retardation, dementia, etc.
High doses of neuroleptics

Depot or parenteral (IM) neuroleptics are more likely to cause NMS
Affective disorders — especially bipolar, or with psychotic features
Rapid neuroleptization
Naive to antipsychotics

 NMS Tidbits

• Treatment of NMS consists of stopping the neuroleptic, supportive measures, and the possible use of **dantrolene** or **bromocriptine**
• NMS has a mortality rate of approximately 15%; early recognition is essential, as is investigating other diagnostic possibilities

Neuroleptic-Induced Tardive Dyskinesia

"CAN BET CLAIM"

Choreiform movements — rapid and jerky
Athetoid movements — slow and sinuous, snake-like
Neuroleptic exposure for at least 3 months

Bucco-lingual
Extremities } sites to check
Trunk

Cognitive disorders
Ladies — the incidence is higher in women
Age increases risk
Interval — longer period of use increases risk
Mood disorder — also non-psychotic disorders
} factors that increase the risk of TD

 TD Tidbits

• Tardive Dyskinesia (TD) is thought to be due to dopamine receptor supersensitivity resulting from prolonged blockade of receptor sites
• Any direct or indirect dopamine agonist can cause TD: some non-psychiatric medications are: **metoclopramide, promethazine, trimethobenzamide, thiethylperazine, trifluopromazine, levodopa, dilantin, antihistamines** and **sympathomimetics,**
• TD can occur without exposure to neuroleptics; it is seen in other disorders, but is not called *neuroleptic-induced* in these cases
• When the dose of neuroleptic medication is decreased, a **withdrawal dyskinesia** can result; similarly, increased doses of neuroleptics can temporarily mask TD
• TD can occasionally manifest as irregular breathing or swallowing
• There is no definite treatment of TD; management includes:
   • a rating scale (**AIMS**) for periodic examination (e.g. every 3-6 months)
   • reducing the dosage or switching to a newer antipsychotic once TD is detected; many medications have been reported to reduce TD (e.g. benzodiazepines, mood stabilizers)

Clozapine Side Effects

"WATCH PREVENTS LOSS"

Weight gain
Agranulocytosis
Temperature elevation (transient)
Collapse — when starting drug (avoid benzodiazepines)
Headaches

Pregnancy — fetal concentration higher than maternal blood levels
Rhinitis
Eosinophilia — may occur at beginning of treatment
Ventricular arrhythmia — torsade de pointes
Enuresis
NMS — has an altered presentation (i.e. fewer EPS)
T wave inversion
Sexual — libido and erectile difficulties are the most common

Leucocytosis (tends to be transient)
OCD — symptoms may worsen
Seizures — risk is dose related
Sialorrhea — also gagging and trouble swallowing

 Clozapine Tidbits

• Weekly WBC and differential are required
• Agranulocytosis is a risk with any medication; always ask about sore throat, fever, sores around the mouth & generalized weakness
• The risk of agranulocytosis is less than 2%; this must be monitored closely and the drug stopped immediately if it is present
• Blood pressure and heart rate may increase when clozapine is first started; the trade name for this medication is Clozaril
• Clozapine has less of an affinity for the D_2 receptor and more for the D_1 and D_4 receptors as well as acting at $5HT_2$ and α_1 sites
• Clozapine causes few incidents of dystonia or parkinsonism
• Tardive dyskinesia and akathisia occur infrequently

Olanzapine Side Effects

"PUT WHERE?"

Pain
Uric acid levels increase
Transaminase levels increase

Weight gain
Headaches
Energy decrease (fatigue)
Rhinitis
Eosinophilia (transient)

 Olanzapine Tidbits

• Weekly blood work is not required; the trade name is Zyprexa
• Drowsiness and anticholinergic side effects are the most common
• Don't confuse with *olsalazine* (used in ulcerative colitis)

Risperidone Side Effects

"HEPATIC"

Headaches
Ejaculatory disturbances (retrograde)
Paresthesias
Agitation, **A**nxiety
Tachycardia (due to hypotension)
Insomnia
Compulsions may worsen if OCD is present

 Risperidone Tidbits

• Weekly blood work is not required; the trade name is Risperdal
• Akathisia and orthostatic hypotension are common side effects
• Of the three atypical antipsychotics, risperidone causes more EPS

Antidepressant Indications

"BASIC BOD SUPPLIES"

Bipolar Depression — acute and prophylactic treatment
Agoraphobia
Smoking cessation
Impulsive behavior
Cataplexy reduction (temporary loss of muscle tone)

Bulimia
Obsessive-Compulsive Disorder
Dysthymic Disorder

Secondary depression in other psychiatric illnesses
Unipolar Depression — acute and prophylactic treatment
Panic Disorder, **P**osttraumatic Stress Disorder
Pain management
Ladies' disorders — Premenstrual Syndrome
Insomnia
Enuresis
Sexual function — premature ejaculation

 Antidepressant Tidbits

• These indications cover both the SSRIs and heterocyclic non-selective antidepressants (including the tricyclics — TCAs)
• In the above list, indications have been demonstrated for only one or two medications (e.g. fluoxetine for smoking cessation)
• Although SSRIs inhibit serotonin reuptake, this has an effect on other neurotransmitter systems (e.g norepinephrine, dopamine, etc.)
• Antidepressants can induce manic episodes and rapid cycling in Bipolar Disorder; although any antidepressant can cause this, tricyclics and MAOIs are among the most likely to do so
• Doxepin can diminish peptic ulcer disease (via histamine blockade)
• Therapeutic plasma levels for many tricyclics are available; up to a 50-fold variation can be seen among those taking the same dosage

Side Effects of TCAs

"NO BOWEL SOUNDS"

Nausea & vomiting
Obesity — usually only a moderate increase in weight

Blurred vision
Orthostatic hypotension
Widening of the QRS complex
Ejaculatory disturbances (impaired sexual function)
Lethargy

Sinus tachycardia
Overdose is particularly dangerous due to cardiac toxicity
Urinary hesitancy
Narrow-angle glaucoma can be precipitated
Dry mucous membranes
Seizure threshold is decreased

 TCA Tidbits

• **TCA** often denotes tricyclic and tetracyclic antidepressants, which are also known as **heterocyclic antidepressants (HCA)**
• TCAs affect many neurotransmitter systems and can cause a diverse array of side effects
• TCAs are lethal in overdose; deaths have been reported at amounts only 3 times the daily therapeutic dose
• TCAs can have an antiarrhythmic effect
• **Clomipramine** is indicated for OCD; **amoxapine** has a neuroleptic action due to its dopamine blockade, and can cause any of the neuroleptic side effects (including tardive dyskinesia)
• TCAs can precipitate manic episodes or rapid cycling
• Plasma levels are available for some TCAs
• Vegetative symptoms (especially sleep and appetite) are often the first to normalize with TCAs (sometimes as soon as 7 days)
• The dosage needs to be both increased and decreased slowly
• Warn patients to get up slowly from standing or lying positions

Side Effects of SSRIs

"THE NEW AGE"

Tremors

Headaches

Euphoria — induce manic episodes in Bipolar Mood Disorder*

Nervousness — agitation, dizziness, restlessness, insomnia

Endocrine — SIADH and galactorrhea have been reported

Weight change (often loss; chronic use may cause weight gain)

Anorgasmia and other sexual side effects

Gastrointestinal upset

Excretions — sweating and rhinitis

 SSRI Tidbits

* SSRIs induce considerably fewer manic episodes than do TCAs
• SSRIs are first-line medications for treating depressive episodes (except for the melancholic type) and have many other uses
• SSRIs are safer in overdose (unless combined with others drugs)
• The starting dose for SSRIs is often the therapeutic dose
• **Sertraline** has the least effect on the P450 metabolizing enzymes
• The duration of **fluoxetine** makes missed doses less of a worry
• **Fluvoxamine** is the least protein-bound of the SSRIs
• **Paroxetine** is the SSRI most likely to be sedating, making it more useful for insomnia and decreasing anxiety
• When added to each other or other serotonergic drugs, SSRIs can cause a **serotonin syndrome**, a hypermetabolic state with: sweating, chills, nausea, vomiting, diarrhea, restlessness, myoclonus, insomnia, agitation and possibly delirium; treatment involves supportive measures and possibly **cyproheptadine**
• Occasional neurologic side effects can be seen such as: akathisia, dystonias and dyskinesias
• SSRIs can cause or worsen extrapyramidal side effects when combined with neuroleptics
• SSRIs may cause coronary vasoconstriction or slow the SA node
• A withdrawal syndrome has been reported — may need to taper

Side Effects of Nefazodone
"HEAD BIDS"

Hypotension
Edema — in higher doses
Asthenia — weakness, fatigue
Dry mouth

Bradycardia
Insomnia
Dizziness
Somnolence — more common than insomnia

 Nefazodone Tidbits

• Nefazodone (Serzone) has a dual action — it inhibits serotonin
($5HT_2$) receptors and is also a serotonin reuptake blocker

Side Effects of Venlafaxine
"DAD SINGS"

Diastolic BP increases — may remain elevated
Anorexia — may result in weight loss
Dry mouth

Sexual — impotence, ejaculatory and orgasmic
Insomnia
Nervousness
Gastrointestinal — nausea & vomiting
Sweating

 Venlafaxine Tidbits

• Venlafaxine (Effexor) is a serotonin norepinephrine reuptake inhibitor (SNRI); it may have a faster onset of action than other drugs

Side Effects of Buproprion

"A SPIN"

Agitation

Seizures — in higher doses

Psychosis — can exacerbate psychotic disorders

Insomnia, Irritability

Nausea

 Buproprion Tidbits

• Buproprion is a distinct antidepressant classified as a selective dopamine reuptake inhibitor (SDRI)
• Buproprion is marketed as Wellbutrin; it is unavailable in Canada
• Buproprion is active only in the CNS, it does not affect the heart, liver, kidneys, cause weight gain or interfere with sexual functioning
• Bulimic patients appear to be at higher risk for seizures; the incidence of seizures increases with a total daily dose over 450mg
• Buproprion may have a use in ADHD

Side Effects of Mirtazapine

"LOADS"

Lipid — level of cholesterol increases

Obesity — weight gain reported more often than weight loss

ALT increases (alanine aminotransferase — a liver enzyme)

Dry mouth

Sedation

 Mirtazapine Tidbits

• Mirtazapine is marketed as Remeron; it is a noradrenergic/specific serotonin antidepressant (NaSSA); it is unavailable in Canada
• No significant EKG changes have been reported; it is unlikely to be toxic in overdose (but can be a concern if part of a mixed overdose)

Electroconvulsive Therapy — ECT

Indications — "CRAMPS"

Catatonia — in schizophrenia, mood disorders & medical conditions

Resistant depression

Acute suicide risk that cannot be managed otherwise

Mania that is unresponsive to pharmacologic management

Psychotic depression; Post-partum depression

Schizophrenia — early onset, and with a preponderance of positive symptoms that are unresponsive to medication

Side Effects — "A MATCH"

Anesthetic complications

Memory difficulties — anterograde more affected than retrograde

Arrhythmias

Tardive seizures — more common with preexisting conditions

Confusion

Headache — can be severe

Relative Contraindications — "FISH CAN"

Fractures of cervical spine

Intracranial pressure increases

Space-occupying lesions

Hypertension

Cardiac events — e.g. recent myocardial infarction

Anesthetic — e.g. malignant hyperthermia, severe arthritis

Neurologic events — e.g. evolving strokes, unexplained symptoms

Side Effects of MAOIs

"PRIME SHOW"

Pyridoxine deficiency (vitamin B$_6$) — may need to take supplements
Renal — urinary hesitancy or retention
Insomnia
Myoclonus
Edema — usually seen around the ankles

Sexual — anorgasmia or impotence are the most common effects
Hypertensive crises — with the ingestion of **tyramine**
Orthostatic hypotension — the original use for MAOIs
Weight gain

 MAOI Tidbits

• MAOIs are indicated for use in: Major Depressive Episodes (especially with marked anxiety or atypical features), Dysthymic Disorder, Social Phobias, Eating Disorders & Anxiety Disorders
• **Tranylcypromine** has an amphetamine-like action; tolerance has been reported with its use; it is a non-hydrazine MAOI with a more reversible inhibition of the MAO enzyme
• **Phenelzine** and **isocarboxazid** are hydrazine MAOIs; these drugs irreversibly inhibit MAO enzymes (there are A and B subtypes)
• **Selegiline** is a specific inhibitor of the MAO$_B$ enzyme subtype and is used for the treatment of Parkinson's disease
• Hepatotoxicity and psychosis are rare side effects of MAOIs
• Regeneration of the MAO enzyme takes up to 14 days
• MAOIs cause hypotension, but have fewer cardiovascular side effects than TCAs, especially on conduction and heart rate
• The MAOI diet is crucial to explain to patients — a consultation with a nutritionist may be helpful; there is a special MAOI diet for patients in hospital; this diet must be continued for at least 2 weeks after stopping an MAOI
• When MAOIs are stopped abruptly, a withdrawal syndrome may develop (agitation, nightmares, myoclonic jerks, palpitations, etc.)
• MAO enzyme activity (measured in platelets) should ideally be inhibited by 80% to yield a therapeutic result

Restrictions of MAOIs

"PASS BY ALL MEANS"

Pickled or smoked foods — especially herring
Aged cheeses — cause 80% of hypertensive crises
Soup stocks & soy sauce
Sausages — especially air-dried

Beans — in particular, fava beans
Yeast supplements — e.g. Marmite

Alcohol — beer and wine (especially Chianti)
Liver — chicken & beef
L-Aspartame — artificial sweetener (contains phenylalanine)

MAOIs — other drugs that have this action are SSRIs, clomipramine
Epinephrine — use with caution in allergic reactions
Anesthetics — may prolong sedation or hypotension
Narcotics — particularly **demerol** and **dextromethorphan**
Sympathomimetics — **phenylephrine, phenylpropanolamine,
              pseudoephedrine, amphetamines and ephedrine**

 MAOI Tidbits

• These restrictions apply to the traditional MAOIs — **phenelzine,
tranylcypromine** and **isocarboxazid**; a new category called RIMA
(Reversible Inhibitors of Monoamine oxidase A) have less severe
dietary restrictions; **moclobemide** is the first agent from this class
• The active ingredient in foods is called **tyramine**; it acts as a
pressor agent and can cause a **hypertensive crisis (**symptoms of a
hypertensive crisis include: severe headache — feels like "head
being ripped off", stiff neck, sweating, nausea and vomiting)
• Hypertensive crises can be treated with sodium nitroprusside or
nitro paste; nifedipine has been used but drops BP too precipitously
• Encourage patients to wear *medic-alert bracelets* or *chains*
and to carry wallet-sized cards containing dietary restrictions
• Due to the short half-life, multiple daily dosing is required

Side Effects of Lithium

"THE MAGIC WAND"

Tremor

Hypothyroidism

EKG changes — flattened or inverted T waves

Muscle weakness

Acne

Gastrointestinal — nausea, vomiting and diarrhea

Increased weight

Cardiac arrhythmias — most common with pre-existing illnesses

White blood cell counts increase (leucocytosis)

Alopecia areata

Neurologic — memory impairment, slowed reaction times, etc.

Diabetes insipidus

 Lithium Tidbits

• Lithium is indicated for the acute and prophylactic treatment of bipolar mood disorders

• Other uses include: major depressive disorder, schizoaffective disorder, schizophrenia (in conjunction with a neuroleptic), disorders where impulsivity is a prominent feature, and some general medical conditions (e.g. cluster headaches)

• Lithium is extremely dangerous when taken in an overdose, and can result in permanent brain damage; it is one of the few psychiatric drugs that can be removed by dialysis

• **Ebstein's anomaly** (of the tricuspid heart valve) is thought to be due to lithium administration in the first trimester of pregnancy

• Lithium is less efficacious for manic episodes with mixed, dysphoric or rapid cycling features

• Levels are drawn 12 hours after the last dose and are also taken 5 days after dosage changes; levels for acute episodes are: 1.0 - 1.2 mEq/L; maintenance levels are between 0.60 - 1.0 mEq/L

• Lithium can be used to augment antidepressants and neuroleptics

Side Effects of Carbamazepine
"HEADS AND TAILS"

Hepatitis — hypersensitivity and cholestatic types
Exfoliative dermatitis and other dermatologic problems
Aplastic anemia
Diploplia
Sedation

Agranulocytosis
Nausea & vomiting
Diarrhea

Teratogenic effects — craniofacial, spina bifida
Ataxia
Induction of hepatic metabolism
Leukopenia
Slows cardiac conduction

 Carbamazepine Tidbits

• Carbamazepine is indicated for the control of partial complex seizures (temporal lobe), grand mal (generalized tonic-clonic) and mixed seizure patterns
• Where **kindling** occurs, carbamazepine is thought to be particularly effective (kindling is defined as repeated subthreshold stimuli that eventually generate an action potential)
• Kindling may occur in the temporal lobes as part of the pathophysiology of mood disorders, hence the rationale for the use of anticonvulsants for these conditions
• Carbamazepine has many other medical uses including: trigeminal neuralgia, tabes dorsalis, migraine headaches, etc.
• Carbamazepine is marketed as Tegretol in the USA and Canada
• Carbamazepine induces its own metabolism, which needs to be monitored (as well as liver function tests, blood cell counts, etc.)
• Carbamazepine also induces metabolism of other drugs metabolized by the cytochrome P-450 enzyme system

Side Effects of Valproate

"WATCH SANTA DROP"

Weight changes
Ammonia levels can increase
Teratogenic effects — neural tube defects, cleft lip, slowed growth
Cholecystitis
Hepatotoxicity — liver enzyme elevation

Sedation
Alopecia
Nausea & vomiting
Tremor
Ataxia

Dysarthria
Rashes
Oligomenorrhea and other menstrual changes
Pancreatitis

| 📖 | Valproate Tidbits

• Valproate is approved as an antiseizure medication for simple and complex absence seizures, and for multiple seizure types that include absence seizures
• It has a wide variety of other uses for medical illnesses
• In psychiatry, it is used for bipolar mood disorders and seems to have a particular use in rapid cycling mood disorders and in mixed states (the coexistence of both manic and depressive symptoms)
• Other psychiatric uses include: reduction of aggression, and augmentation of antidepressants and neuroleptics
• Hepatotoxicity can occur in children under age 2, especially if they have seizure disorders, metabolic disorders or mental retardation
• Valproate is thought to work by increasing levels of GABA
• Valproate can be combined with lithium and carbamazepine
• Valproate is marketed as Depakene and Depakote in the USA, and as Epival in Canada

Side Effects of Benzodiazepines

"ADDED TRAP"

Ataxia

Dizziness

Drowsiness

Erectile dysfunction — other sexual side effects reported

Disinhibition

Teratogenic — suspected to cause cleft palate

Respiratory conditions can worsen

Amnesia — anterograde memory difficulties

Paradoxical aggression

Benzodiazepine Tidbits

• Benzodiazepines are very effective anxiety-reducing agents and are used in many psychiatric conditions: insomnia, anxiety disorders, depression (**alprazolam**), mania (**clonazepam**) and **akathisia**

• Benzodiazepines have potent anti-seizure properties

• Due to the development of tolerance, these medications should be administered on a time-limited basis; dose and duration are the two variables that determine whether tolerance develops

• High-potency benzodiazepines cause more withdrawal problems

• These drugs are not usually lethal in overdose unless taken in combination with other medications or alcohol

• Benzodiazepine withdrawal can become life threatening; the symptoms are similar to alcohol and barbiturate withdrawal

• Rebound anxiety can occur with abrupt cessation, or if the dosing interval is longer than the drug half-life

• Combination with **clozapine** (a dibenzodiazepine neuroleptic) may cause severe complications; avoid use in sleep apnea

• Benzodiazepines increase total sleep time, but decrease stage 3 & 4 sleep and suppress REM sleep; this can lead to a rebound of REM sleep and insomnia when the medication is stopped

• Parenteral forms are available for diazepam (i.v.), lorazepam (i.m.) and midazolam (i.v.)

• Mild anticholinergic side effects can occur

HIV Encephalopathy

"HOPE AND SAD TIMES"

Half of HIV⁺ patients have neuropsychiatric complications
Opportunistic infections are common
Personality changes often appear first
EEG changes — shows generalized slowing

Atrophy of cerebral cortex
Neuronal cell loss
Dementia — subcortical in nature

Substance abuse ⎫
Anxiety ⎬ the most common psychiatric manifestations
Depression ⎭

Treatments may slow development (e.g. antiretrovirals, AZT)
Involvement of significant others and community supports
Memory loss impacts on treatment (e.g. forgetting appointments)
Effects of psychiatric medication are magnified; use smaller doses
Suicide risk increases dramatically

 HIV Tidbits

• HIV seropositivity or AIDS can mimic any psychiatric condition; syphilis was called the "great imitator" due to its numerous possible physical manifestations; HIV also has this capability
• In practice, the most common conditions are anxiety, depression, substance-related disorders, psychosis, delirium and dementia
• Patients are at risk for maladaptive behaviors and suicide when informed about seropositivity and with the onset of AIDS
• Some patients in higher-risk groups develop an obsession with being seropositive and manifest several signs and symptoms (despite having negative blood tests)
• With all due respect to the the research being carried out, education and prevention remain the two best strategies at present
• Always ask patients about intravenous drug use

Panic Attack Mnemonic

"People sweat, choke and shake for fear nobody can hear deadly death summon."

P — palpitations
S — sweating
C — choking
A — abdominal distress
S — shaking
F — fear of losing control
F — fear of dying
N — numbness
C — chest pain
H — hot flashes
D — dizziness
D — derealization or depersonalization
S — shortness of breath

Panic Attack mnemonic by:
**Dr. Bryan Weinstein
Birmingham, MI**

Medical Differential Diagnosis

• **Cardiac**
arrhythmias, angina, myocardial infarction, cardiac tamponade, aortic dissection, mitral valve prolapse

• **Respiratory**
asthma, pneumonia, hyperventilation, pulmonary embolus

• **GI**
gastro-esophageal reflux, peptic ulcer disease, cholecystitis

• **Endocrine/Metabolic**
hyperthyroidism, thyroid storm, hypoglycemia, pheochromocytoma

• **Substance Use**
cocaine, amphetamines, caffeine, other stimulants

General Principles Regarding Capacity Assessments

• Incompetence is a legal term; incapacity is what is relevant to the practice of medicine
• There are several areas in which capacity assessments are done
• Each area of capacity is addressed individually; the threshold of competence varies (for example, a patient may be incapable of managing finances but still be capable of consenting to treatment)
• Capacity involves understanding the nature and consequences of a specific act

Suggested Procedure for Determining Financial Capacity

• Inform the patient of the reason for your visit/assessment
• Use **plain** English; document the patient's responses

Screening Questions Regarding Financial Capacity
• Awareness of sources of income (with amounts) and debts/bills/expenses (with amounts)
• Ability to give the prices of common objects
• Ability to figure out the change expected for purchases
• Ability to describe common banking procedures

Assess the Following to Determine Financial Capacity
• Perform a mental status exam (especially orientation, thought content & process, perception and cognition)
• Are there any documented problems with estate management?
• Is the patient aware of having any difficulties with finances?
• What is the patient's appreciation of being financially incompetent?
• Is the patient aware of having any debts, bills or expenses?
• Can the patient cope with daily financial tasks?
• What sources of collateral information are available?
• Has assistance been required in the past?
• What support is presently available on an ongoing basis?
• What is the patient's preference for estate management?
• What is the patient's understanding of power of attorney?
• Has power of attorney been assigned previously?

Assessment of the Capacity for Consent to Treatment

Suggested Procedure for Determining Capacity:
• Inform the patient of the reason for your visit/assessment
• Inform the patient of his or her diagnosis
• Outline the risks and benefits of your proposed treatment
• Outline the risks and benefits of alternate treatments
• Explain the risks and likely consequences of receiving no treatment
• Use *plain* English!
• Ask the patient to repeat what his or her understanding is, and what he or she heard you say
• Perform a mental status exam (it is especially important to test orientation, thought content & process, perception and cognition)
• Document the patient's responses

Assess the Following to Determine Capacity:
• What is the patient's choice?
• What is the patient's rationale for making that choice?
• What are the likely consequences of exercising the choice?
• Can the patient weigh the pros and cons of various alternatives?
• What is the patient's understanding of the medical problem?
• What is the patient's understanding of your recommendations and rationale?
• What consequences does the patient foresee from the treatment you have proposed?
• What consequences does the patient foresee from NOT receiving treatment?
• Can the patient make a commitment to a choice?

If You Deem the Patient Incapable —
• Document your interaction with the patient completely
• Inform the patient (verbally and in writing)
• Ask for a second opinion (colleague, psychiatrist)
• Ask for legal advice (lawyer, rights advisor)
• Involve the family as soon and as completely as possible
• Obtain substitute consent

The Folstein Mini-Mental State Exam

Orientation   Score

• What is the — (day) (date) (month) (season) (year)?   /5
• Where you are now? (building) (floor) (town)
                            (state) (country)   /5

Registration

• List 3 objects at one-second intervals, then ask
the patient to repeat all 3; give one point for each
correct answer given **on the first trial**; repeat this
until the patient can recite all 3 items   /3

Attention & Calculation

• Serial 7's Test up to 5 subtractions (starting with
100 - 7); alternatively ask the patient to spell
WORLD backwards (D - L - R - O - W)   /5

Recall

• Ask the patient to recite the above 3 items   /3

Language

• Show the patient a *watch* and a *pen* and ask the
patient to name these items   /2

• Ask the patient to repeat the following statement:
"*No ifs, ands or buts.*"   /1

• Ask the patient to follow these commands:
Take a piece of paper in your right hand (1 pt.)
Fold it in half (1 pt.)
Place it on the floor (1 pt.)   /3

• Read and follow this command
CLOSE YOUR EYES   /1

Score

• Write a sentence:

_____

_____

_____

/1

• Copy the following diagram:

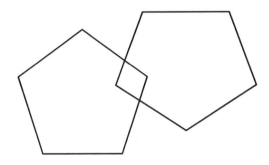

/1

Total Score

/30

Tidbits on Interviewing Skills

Because psychiatric diagnoses are made in interview situations, developing skills in obtaining information is crucial to this process. Especially relevant to assessments are the following considerations:

• A psychiatric interview is not a conversation, but an active period of questioning and observation. All aspects of the person being interviewed are subject to scrutiny: body odors, unusual movements, grooming habits, etc. Areas that might be tactfully avoided in social situations are pursued in assessments to further the understanding of that person.
• Be interested!! Pursue hints, suggestions and insinuations.
• Psychiatric interviews allow the privilege of asking about personal matters and making repeated inquiries for further information.
• Exude a neutral, calm and objective manner. All aspects of patients' lives (sexual, religious, fantasy) are relevant. Information involving sensitive areas is best obtained using a straightforward, nonjudgmental demeanor. Your task is to understand patients and empathize with them. An attitude of curiosity and acceptance helps to facilitate this exchange.
• Be flexible. Adjust your tone, vocabulary and types of questions to suit the patient.
• At regular intervals, take a break to check your understanding of patients' problems with them. This clearly conveys your interest, and will often help clarify which areas need further questioning.
• Attend to the comfort of your patients. Provide tissues, water, etc., to see that their needs are met. Taking care of these preliminary matters expresses empathy and helps avoid interruptions.

References for Interviewing Skills
Psychiatric Interviewing: The Art of Understanding
S. Shea, M.D.
W.B. Saunders; Philadelphia, 1988

The Clinical Interview Using DSM-IV
Volume 1: The Fundamentals
E. Othmer, M.D., Ph.D & S. Othmer, Ph.D
American Psychiatric Press Inc.; Washington D.C., 1994

The First Interview — Revised for DSM-IV
J. Morrison, M.D.
The Guilford Press; New York, 1994

Sample Mental Status Report

P. S. is a 33-year-old, single, unemployed male brought to the emergency department after accosting patrons for cigarettes in a shopping center.

- Appearance: tattered jeans, soiled sneakers and a sweater which seemed too heavy for the warm weather; unshaven with unwashed hair and had tobacco stains on his hands
- Behavior: restless during the interview, stood up twice to look in the ashtray, but was able to be directed back to his seat; fidgeted constantly with his lighter and appeared distracted
- Cooperation: moderately interested in the interview; information limited but considered reliable; eye contact was intermittent
- Speech: spontaneous and fluent, spoke in a low voice and had occasional difficulty naming people, places, and events
- Thought Content: answered questions grudgingly with little elaboration; spontaneously spoke about the injustices he'd suffered by "the system" and specified how today's events were part of a scheme to persecute him; this belief was strongly held throughout the interview and unwavering in intensity
- Thought Process: his thoughts were logically connected with a restricted flow of ideas and one episode of thought derailment
- Affect & Mood: his emotional expression ranged from mildly sullen to moderately irritable; he became hostile when he was told he would have to remain in the hospital; he described his mood as "pissed off" and rated it as one on a ten point scale
- Perception: experienced continual, clearly formed auditory hallucinations throughout the interview which told him he was stupid to get detained at the hospital and he should find a way to get released immediately; he did not report other perceptual disturbances
- Suicide/Homicide: no thoughts or plans for self-harm; he wishes to assault one of the officers who brought him into hospital
- Insight & Judgment: deemed impaired; he denies he was bothering anyone or that he has any need for hospitalization or treatment
- Cognition:
- alert and fully conscious throughout the interview
- oriented to person, day, date, month, year, season and place
- able to register three objects on the second attempt and recall two of them about four minutes later (despite prompting, he couldn't recall the third); remote memory was impaired for historical details obtained from hospital record (dates and events)
- digit span five forward, four backward; attempted two serial seven subtractions, both were incorrect (97, 87), then stopped this task
- declined to answer questions testing general knowledge, abstraction ability, proverb interpretation or hypothetical situations

Parking Lot Personality Assessment

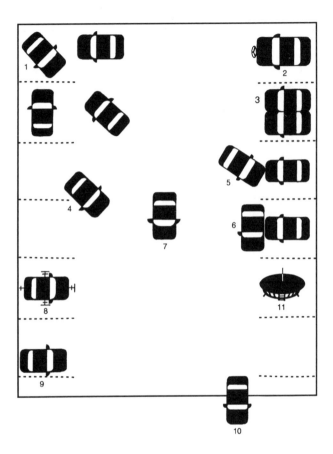

Key

1. Paranoid — Cornered again!!
2. Narcissist — Largest car; prominent hood ornament
3. Dependent — Needs other cars to feel sheltered
4. Passive-Aggressive — Angles car to take two spaces
5. Borderline — Rams car of ex-lover
6. Antisocial — Obstructs other cars
7. Histrionic — Parks in center of lot for dramatic effect
8. Obsessive — Perfect alignment in parking spot
9. Avoidant — Hides in corner
10. Schizoid — Lives on the edge (or sidelines in this case)
11. Schizotypal — Intergalactic parking

Occupational Personality Assessment

Senior Management

President
Narcissist

Vice-President
Paranoid

Personnel
Borderline

Middle Management

Advertising Histrionic	**Legal Department** Antisocial
Research Schizotypal	**Customer Service** Passive-Aggressive

Workforce (with preferred hours)

Dependent (Whenever Told)	**Obsessive** (Day and Night)
Schizoid (Nights Only)	**Avoidant** (Undesirable Shifts)

Mental "Status Symbols"

Serial 7's Champion	Concrete Thinker	Tangential Speech	Labile Mood
Paranoid Ideas	Rigid Thinking	Completely Oriented	Financially Competent
Thought Broadcasting	Thought Insertion	Flight of Ideas	Thought Blocking
Visual Hallucination	Auditory Hallucination	Olfactory Hallucination	Gustatory Hallucination
Nihilistic Delusion	Somatic Fixation	Tactile Hallucination	Erotomanic Delusion
	R$_x$		(heart)
Wide Range of Affect	Knows Correct Age	Loud Speech	Thought Derailment
(masks)	(cake)	(megaphone)	(clapboard)
Unusual Attire	Well Dressed & Groomed	Knowledge Intact	Knowledge Deficient
(lamp)	(penguin)	(checkmark)	(door)

Descriptive Shorthand

Complicated History

Easily Frustrated

Talkative

Day Dreamer

Competitive

Family Scapegoat

Politely Persistent

Believes in Reincarnation

Avoids Responsibility

Oriented

Lives Alone

Divorced

Married

Separated

Reconciliation Impossible

Hereditary Tendencies

Mature Ego Defenses

Improved in Therapy

Therapeutic Resistance

Primitive Ego Defenses

A Survivor

Rorschach Survivor

Childhood Survivor

MMPI Survivor

Cognitive Survivor

Inhibited

Liberal

Assertive

Confabulator

Conservative

Genogrammania

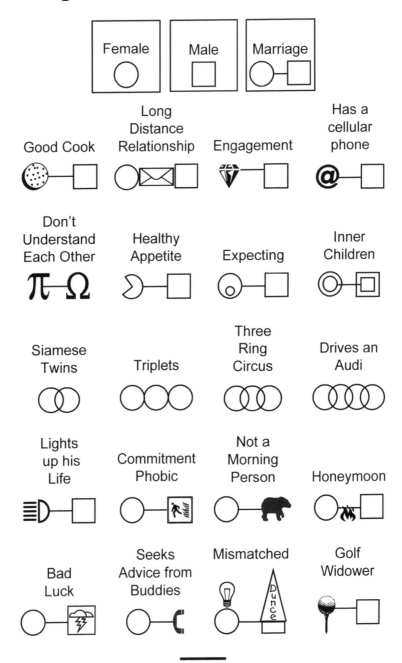

Tries to
Patch
Things Up

Having
A
Fling

Messy
Divorce

Marital
Therapy

Troubled
Relationship

Co-
Dependent

Cow
Dependent

Made for
Each Other

Impending
Separation

Legal
Separation

Hopeful
Relationship

C & W
Lovers

Restraining
Order

Valentine
Sweethearts

Reconciling

Sees
Issues
Clearly

Long
Courtship

Distant
Relationship

Ambivalent

Still has
a few
Hang-ups

Needs an
Umpire

All's Fair
in Love
(relatively)

Plays Hard
to Get

Caught on
the Rebound

Brain Calipers
A Guide to a Successful
Mental Status Exam

Brain Calipers: A Guide to a Successful Mental Status Exam
provides a comprehensive and enjoyable overview of the
mental status exam. Features include:
• Individually referenced **DSM-IV** diagnostic criteria that
pertain to findings on the Mental Status Exam
• Coverage of each aspect of the MSE in an individual chapter
with definitions, examples, and explanations outlining the
relevance of specific findings
• Sample questions to ask in each section of the MSE
• An "edutainment" approach with over forty illustrations,
humorous articles, mnemonics and helpful summary diagrams

392 pages, soft-cover, ISBN 0-9680324-3-5

DISORDERED PERSONALITIES

A PRIMER

Disordered Personalities: A Primer

This book a comprehensive and entertaining introduction to the DSM-IV personality disorders. The information is presented in an organized and readable format, with humor contributing an effective and entertaining presentation. A unique approach is used by illustrating "textbook" concepts with examples that all readers will enjoy.

Features include:
- Explanations of diagnostic and theoretical principles
- Thorough coverage of each personality disorder
- Summaries of past personality disorders
- DSM-IV diagnostic criteria

288 pages, hard-cover, ISBN 0-9680324-0-0

This anthology contains satirical articles and caricatures from the **Psycho-Illogical Bulletin**. This unique volume is an excellent resource for teaching classes, speaking engagements and livening up bulletin boards.

"I had a whale of a time reading this book. Sign me up, I'm hooked"

Captain Everett Ahab, Sturgeon General

192 pages, soft-cover, ISBN 0-9680324-4-3

Presentation Sets

Color presentation graphics are available as 35mm slides (standard size) and overhead transparencies. These original hand-drawn, full-color illustrations cover a wide range of topics in the Behavioral Sciences.

Presentation sets are available for the following topics:
- **Diagnostic and Theoretical Principles**
- **Clinical Conditions (Axis I Disorders)**
- **The Interview and The Mental Status Exam**
- **Personality Disorders (Axis II Disorders)**
- **Ego Defenses**
- **Consultation-Liaison Psychiatry**
- **Childhood Psychiatric Disorders**

The Sadistic and Masochistic Personalities

About the Author

Dave Robinson is a psychiatrist practicing in London, Ontario, Canada. His particular interests are consultation-liaison psychiatry and education. A graduate of the University of Toronto Medical School, he completed a Residency in Family Practice before entering the Psychiatry Residency Program.

His hobbies include the saxophone, computer simulation games, and yes, cycling.

He is a Lecturer in Psychiatry at the University of Western Ontario in London, Canada and was the recipient of the 1996 Award for Excellence in Clinical Clerk Teaching.

About the Artist

Brian Chapman is a resident of Oakville, Ontario, Canada. He was born in Sussex, England and moved to Canada in 1957. His first commercial work took place during W.W. II when he traded drawings for cigarettes while serving in the British Navy. Now retired, Brian was formerly a Creative Director at Mediacom. He continues to freelance and is versatile in a wide range of media. He is a master of the caricature, and his talents are constantly in demand. He doesn't smoke anymore.

Brian is an avid swimmer and trumpeter. He performs regularly (playing the trumpet) in the Toronto area as a member of three bands. He is married to Fanny, a cook, bridge player and crossword puzzle solver extraordinaire.

About Rapid Psychler Press

Rapid Psychler Press was founded in 1994 with the aim of producing resources and materials that further the use of humor in mental health education. In addition to textbooks, Rapid Psychler Press specializes in producing CD-ROMs, slides and overheads for presentations.